LIB051005 R3/78

SIMON FRASER

Unless recalled, all materials

Third Generation R&D

Third Generation R&D
Managing the Link to Corporate Strategy

Philip A. Roussel, Kamal N. Saad,
Tamara J. Erickson

Arthur D. Little, Inc.

Foreword by John F. Magee

Harvard Business School Press
Boston, Massachusetts

© 1991 by Arthur D. Little, Inc.
All rights reserved.
Printed in the United States of America.

95 94 93 92 91   5 4 3 2 1

Library of Congress Cataloging-in-Publication Data

Roussel, Philip A., 1928–
    Third generation R&D : managing the link to corporate strategy /
  Philip A. Roussel, Kamal N. Saad, Tamara J. Erickson ; foreword by
  John F. Magee.
        p.   cm.
    Includes bibliographical references and index.
    ISBN 0-87584-252-6 (hard : acid free paper)
    1. Research, Industrial—Management.   2. Strategic planning.
  I. Saad, Kamal N., 1929–   . II. Erickson, Tamara J., 1954–
  III. Title.   IV. Title: Third generation R & D.   V. Title: Third
  generation R and D.
  T175.5.R68   1991   90-19497
  658.5′7—dc20   . CIP

The paper used in this publication meets the requirements of the
American National Standard for Permanence of Paper for Printed
Library Materials Z39.49—1984.

To our clients and our colleagues;
and to Claudia, Ditha, and Tom,
our partners who endured much and
supported us grandly.

The industrialist who rejects the aid of science is about to be weighed in the balance. He will then be found wanting, and his business will soon pass to other hands. The wise investor will avoid him and his companies.

—Arthur Dehon Little
The Handwriting on the Wall

CONTENTS

Foreword by John F. Magee   ix

Preface   xv

Acknowledgments   xix

Chapter 1   The Link to Strategy   1

Chapter 2   What Are: Technology? Research? Development?   13

Chapter 3   A Framework for Purposeful R&D Management   23

Chapter 4   Top Management and R&D   41

Briefing Paper 1   Technology, Maturation, and Competitive Impact   59

Chapter 5   Evaluating Risks and Rewards   67

Briefing Paper 2   Technological Competitive Position   87

Chapter 6   The R&D Portfolio   93

Chapter 7   Organizing R&D for Results   123

Chapter 8   Beyond Project Management   143

Chapter 9   Getting the Most Out of Your People: Breaking R&D Isolation   163

Chapter 10   The Third Generation Company   175

Afterword   185

Index   187

FOREWORD

This book, *Third Generation R&D: Managing the Link to Corporate Strategy*, is designed to give business leaders and their managers the concepts that will help them manage research and development as a strategic competitive weapon. The value of a business enterprise depends on the level and growth rate of its cash flow; thus, a firm's ability to maintain an advantage in its markets depends on whether the growth in cash flow can be sustained. The goal of strategic management of research and development is to help ensure that the cash flow will be sustained and will continue to grow. Effective management of this kind can help a firm gain and maintain competitive advantages ranging from incremental improvements in product quality or cost to major breakthroughs that create new market opportunities. The management of research and development, however, must be purposeful rather than hopeful or "hands off" and must always be connected with the firm's overall business strategy.

Leaders of business organizations recognize the critical importance of research and development management to their success in guiding their firms to becoming and remaining world-class competitors. In a recent survey, the top five concerns of American chief executives of manufacturing firms were areas in which research and development play key roles: product quality, reduced production costs, the company's future strength, keeping up with new technology, and product development.[1] The executives' concerns were well founded. In the decades ahead, competition will grow increasingly international in character and will focus increasingly on technological strengths. Financial and physical resources, work skills, and technology are highly mobile. The firms that succeed in global competition will be those that employ technology to maintain an edge in product quality and innovation, an advantage in production and marketing productivity, and responsiveness to market interests. This

[1] *Industry Week,* November 20, 1989, p. 12.

success in turn depends on each firm's skill in managing its research
and development effort.

Industrial research and development was born in the early twenti-
eth century. The context was not propitious. In 1899, Charles Duell
resigned as director of the United States Patent Office because, he
said, "Everything that can be invented has been invented." Nevertheless, there were some pioneers. Du Pont established its central research laboratory early in the century. The young and expanding
General Motors Corporation hired Arthur Dehon Little in 1911 to
organize GM's first central laboratory to study the materials used in
GM products. The employees of Little's company provided the initial
temporary staff for the laboratory. Through the early decades of the
century, Little and other promoters of industrial technology faced
widespread skepticism from hardheaded businessmen who saw little
connection between "academic" science and product innovation and
who valued hard assets over intellectual property.

After World War II, research and development emerged as a
widely recognized industrial force. The success of leading firms in
industries such as chemicals, electronics, and pharmaceuticals in exploiting new products for rapid growth in revenues and profits, based
on technical developments, created wide interest in research and development particularly in the United States and Europe and among
emerging Japanese firms. The technical virtuosity embedded in these
new products, however, blinded too many observers to the pragmatic
problem-solving orientation of the most successful research and development efforts. Businessmen, naive about technology, hoped to
buy science and emulate the success of a Du Pont; and aggressive,
sometimes arrogant directors of new, rapidly expanding research
and development functions demanded independence and isolation to
pursue their ideas.

In the decades since, business leaders have been working to find
more effective means to integrate the management of research and
development with the strategic direction of the organization. The
barriers have been substantial. Language and conceptual understanding have been problems. In the United States, in particular, executive
leadership has come up through the marketing or finance functions,
traditionally the most powerful. Training for these functions has not
required scientific literacy. The scientific and engineering community
for its part has viewed business people with suspicion or disdain—as
"hucksters" and "bean counters." Even today there is a widespread

doubt among many scientists and engineers that formal business education can have any useful relevance to their work.

Another source of friction is the issue of reconciling the unpredictability of discovery with the desire to fit technical programs into a framework for the orderly management of the business. Western business executives have been indoctrinated in the concept of management based on measurement. Measurements of activity (for example, sales or units produced) serve as surrogates for measures of productivity. Cost accounting and control systems have been extended into practically every corner of the enterprise. The research and development function, however, has characteristically resisted this pressure for short-term measurable results, because the results most of the time cannot be seen to be counted. Other functions in the business resent the R&D resistance to being held accountable on comparable terms.

A third source of difficulty is a tendency to see the activity of product and process development as linear—that is, as moving straight from research to development to engineering to manufacture to sales. The idea under development is perceived as falling in the sole domain of one function or another until it is tossed over the wall to the next function (or tossed back as unworkable) with a ceremonial washing of the hands in the process: "We've developed the concept of 'wrap-around' TV. It's up to engineering to work out the details."

These issues reflect both causes and symptoms of difficulty in the traditional approach to managing research and development that was widely adopted in the period of euphoria and growth after World War II. The traditional approach, referred to by the authors of this book as first generation R&D management, has been largely intuitive. Research and development is treated as an overhead item, and budgets are set in relation to some business measure (for example, sales) and at a level deemed reasonable by industry practice. Budgets may be projected several years ahead but usually are set annually. Within this budget framework, decisions about areas of concentration and project continuation may be left largely to R&D management. There is no assurance that the R&D organization, left to its own devices, will pursue programs related to business or corporate strategy, either in focus or in degree of innovation and risk.

In response to this unsatisfactory situation, many firms have become somewhat more sophisticated. In second generation, or system-

atic, R&D management, managers outside the R&D area participate
in suggesting or reviewing projects. Although each project, individually, may be consistent with business strategy, the relationship of the
R&D program to overall company strategy is haphazard or incomplete. Some firms subject R&D programs to a rigorous financial
justification process based on net present value. Arguing that research and development projects are investments—as in a sense they
are—corporate management seeks to base their justification on rate
of return or payout. But projecting financial returns on an R&D
project is difficult, especially if the project is focused on achieving a
significant innovation. As a result, the R&D program may be pushed
toward conservative, incremental projects, in which case the results
will be more predictable but the program will have limited strategic
impact.

Clearly, then, there is a need for a thoughtful, genuinely sophisticated approach to R&D management. Interest in a better approach
has been stimulated by four developments. First, many corporate
leaders have moved beyond the financially driven planning characteristic of the 1970s. Second, the success of entrepreneurial, high-
technology companies has excited interest in the potential of technology
to build company value. Third, firms have seen that industry leaders
give high priority to technology management. Fourth, quality and
manufacturing capability are now considered strategic business
weapons. Together these developments have helped create a desire
to manage R&D in a way that is congruent with business strategy.

This book describes how research and development can be managed effectively in a large, complex enterprise to support and enrich
its business strategy. The authors characterize this process as third
generation management, to distinguish it from the primitive hands-
off "strategy of hope" or the somewhat more systematic but incomplete project-management approach. Third generation research and
development management is a continuous interactive process. It demands active dialogue and a sense of partnership in technology
among the leadership of R&D and other key managers focused on
business strategy. This is possible only if all involved undertake to
educate themselves about each other's concerns and perspectives.
This style of R&D management requires regular review of the R&D
project portfolio in relation to product and market strategy. It requires active participation of general management to ensure direction, provide guidance, and mobilize resources.

Third Generation R&D gives the reader practical guidance on how to create an environment in which the right R&D is done and in which R&D is done right to support corporate success. This is not accomplished only by case studies or by examining a few successful companies. Case studies have limited value because the particular conditions of a specific company can probably never be replicated. Rather, the authors present a synthesis of concepts that can be used by any leadership team in any company to make R&D a strategic force in corporate growth and competitiveness.

The authors of *Third Generation R&D* are uniquely qualified to describe the philosophy and process of third generation research and development management. The author team has decades of experience helping companies create strategic technology plans in such diverse industries as automobiles, electronics, biotechnology, computers, processed food, energy, medical technology, chemicals, and pharmaceuticals. The authors have been supported by a score of supporting contributors, who in turn have drawn on the resources of over 1,500 Arthur D. Little consultants who have worked in most of the major industries throughout the developed and developing world. This rich and extensive experience, combined with over a century of contract research for clients, has been the crucible in which the concepts of third generation research and development have been developed, tested, and refined.

John F. Magee
Chairman of the Board
Arthur D. Little, Inc.

PREFACE

This book was born out of our long-held conviction that R&D and technology play a crucial role in ensuring the profitability of companies and from decades of experience with R&D planning and management in countless companies and industries on all continents. Despite the diversity of our experiences, we began to discern one common characteristic: R&D organizations were rarely integrated spiritually or strategically as full and equal partners in the business enterprises whose prosperity they were intended to serve.

In the worst cases we found R&D treated as a line item in the budget, as a tax on the businesses. Its relevance and value were unclear, and its organization was physically and culturally isolated from the mainstream of the businesses. The analogy comes to mind of a family with an eccentric uncle who must be supported but who is best kept out of sight.

In other instances we observed attempts to build bridges between the businesses and R&D. But the traffic across the bridges tended to be messengers with specific missions: "R&D, why can't you move faster?" "Marketing, this is a wonderful new product. Why won't you adopt it?" "Engineering, we sent you the prototype months ago. What's holding you up?" "R&D, justify the millions we have spent on you over the past five years."

More typically we found that businesses perceive R&D as an organization that occasionally produces useful results and as a resource to be tapped for specific accomplishments identified as needs by the businesses and adopted as projects by R&D—a line extension, a new product with features specified by marketing, a cost reduction, an enhancement of quality. An improvement, to be sure, but project-by-project direction is the equivalent of contract R&D, and the process is suboptimal because the full strategic value of the R&D resource is not engaged.

In virtually all instances the companies' formal planning process produced corporate and business strategic plans and a separate R&D

plan whose relationship to business strategies was incomplete and whose contribution to the formation of business strategies was slight. We kept wondering why we rarely saw a single integrated plan in whose creation R&D played a vital role and of which R&D was an inseparable part.

If the unifying theme of our experience—the incomplete connection between the corporation and its businesses and R&D—was common across so many companies, we wondered if the underlying causes might also be common. We accumulated and shared experience, read and studied, traded hypotheses, debated whether the impairments to the realization of full R&D value were the causes of the disconnect or the effects of forces buried even more deeply in the character of the companies. Out of this intellectual ferment we came to the postulate and then the conviction that there are common causes, that certain management, R&D planning, and operational principles seem universally applicable for superior return from investments in R&D, and, *mirabile dictu,* that they are, in concept if not always in practice, simple. At the core of these principles is the integration of R&D into equal partnership with the corporation and its businesses. (Webster; to integrate: to unite so as to form a complete or perfect whole.) We saw our conviction confirmed in some exemplary companies.

There is no single "best" way to superior R&D. There is no prescription, no computer model, no mechanical application of rules that will ensure it. Every company, every competitive environment is unique and in a state of its own unique continuous change. The evolution of an individual company to what we call third generation R&D will be managed according to the specific identity, culture, and will of the company in its individual competitive arena. We do offer to corporate, business, and R&D management guiding principles that our experience argues have universal value. If applied by management with intelligence, sensitivity, determination, and perseverance, they will lead to superior returns from R&D investments. The returns will be expressed in units understood by all business management: superior competitive positions and enhanced earnings and growth.

We have organized the book as follows. We discuss the first and second generations of R&D management, how they were practiced, why and when they were effective, and why they are no longer sufficient. We introduce the guiding principles of third generation R&D expressed in the experience of the Intercontinental Company, a composite company, fictitious but constructed from real-life experience, whose new CEO did not have a technical background yet sensed the need for radical change in the role of his R&D organizations. We then describe the experience of the CEO and his senior managers in adapting the principles to Intercontinental's needs, the processes they adopted, and the vicissitudes they encountered in applying them. We follow this account with discussions of human and operational effectiveness in the prosecution of R&D and conclude with a reprise that reviews the state of Intercontinental two years after beginning the move to third generation R&D.

Coda

The treatment of gender in a book of this nature is a delicate and difficult matter. The authors hope that readers of both genders will accept their intent that the use of the pronoun "he" is in the classical sense of "he" a person, not "he" a male.

ACKNOWLEDGMENTS

More people and organizations have contributed to the creation of this book than we can possibly acknowledge individually by name. In particular they are our clients and our colleagues, whose experience in identifying issues of R&D effectiveness and arriving at innovative solutions provided the foundation and the proving ground for our concepts. The trust and sharing among our colleagues and between all of us and the many companies with which we have worked on R&D matters command our unique respect and gratitude.

Within Arthur D. Little, we offer special acknowledgment to Frederik Van Oene and Nils Bohlin in Brussels and Claus Tiby in Wiesbaden. They made direct contributions to the development of the concept and to the later chapters of this book. Their insight, creativity, and energy made their participation invaluable.

Senior Vice President John Ketteringham, who pioneered the idea of integrating R&D into corporate and business strategy, was an inspiration to all of us. John Magee, chairman of the board of Arthur D. Little, and Senior Vice President Alfred Wechsler provided constant encouragement and occasionally the discipline to ensure that authors busy with the work they most love—working with clients—was not an excuse for tarrying. The creativity and enthusiasm of Jean-Philippe Deschamps of Brussels and Tom Sommerlatte of Wiesbaden are spread throughout the book. Our debt to these colleagues is large.

Other busy Arthur D. Little associates gave of their time and expertise unstintingly: Nancy Smith in the food, beverage, and flavor industries; Steve Rudolph in the chemical and polymer industries and in hands-on, laboratory-based product development; Bruce Thompson of London and Atsu Kokobu of Tokyo in electronics, packaging, and consumer products industries. Skip Irving made important contributions from his excellent work in the pharmaceutical industry. Other colleagues, too numerous to single out by name, shared their experiences in the automotive, ceramics, medical diagnostics, electrical, paint, adhesives, metals, petroleum, and other industries. Their experiences reinforced our confidence in the universality of the principles espoused in this book. To them all we offer lasting thanks.

Bob Mueller, retired chairman of the board and author of many books, somehow forced himself through the early, clumsy drafts and offered wise, witty, and valuable counsel.

A book of this nature inevitably demands research. Herb Taylor energetically, intelligently, and productively undertook the research assignments and, even though he really wanted to be working with clients instead, did it with a smile.

With flair, dedication, and skill, our overworked secretaries, Jeanne Marasca, Maki Gilles, and Claire Murray, suffered through draft after draft, coordinating the work of authors constantly on the move.

Celia Doremus of Arthur D. Little's corporate communications department skillfully and delicately but firmly managed time issues. Somehow she knows how to make discipline fun.

Richard Luecke, our editor, had the confidence to support and encourage us when all we had to show him was scarcely more than a vision. His trust, patience, and gentle discipline helped impel us from vision to drafts to revisions to refinements to a finished product of which we all feel proud.

Third Generation R&D

Chapter 1

The Link to Strategy

The R&D imperative for industry has never been more compelling. Virtually all industry feels the impact of both increased competition—much of it technically based—and the accelerated pace of technological challenge and change.

Many companies cannot increase their R&D investment fast enough to compensate for the international R&D challenges they face. The answer cannot simply be to spend "more" on R&D, because more can never be enough. The solution, rather, must be to deploy R&D investments more effectively—that is, more strategically and more efficiently.

In his macroeconomic evaluation of the contribution by R&D to corporate profitability, Bruce Old demonstrated a strong positive relationship between long-term profitability and the proportion of cash flow that a company is willing to put at risk in R&D and in the productive capital investment that ensues.[1] Though few will dispute his conclusion, the issue facing individual companies is not macroeconomic; it is less how much to spend on R&D than how to spend allocated resources well. That is the central focus of this book.

Deciding what R&D to undertake and at what level of resources and priority is one of the most complex and critical decisions general management faces today. Notice the emphasis on general management, for the truth in today's environment is that R&D planning is too important to be left solely to researchers. Increasingly, corporate management is realizing that the most decisive factor in the overall success of R&D is the selection of strategically worthwhile R&D goals and that the allocation of resources and establishment of policies needed to execute the goals must be determined by *senior management* in a timely and effective fashion. These determinants of success demand the participation—the partnership—of business, corporate, and R&D management.

There are other pressing reasons for focusing on effective and efficient R&D. One has to do with the growing limitation on the

1

availability of technical talent. The National Science Foundation reported that the United States will face a serious shortfall of technically trained talent as the 1990s moves on. By the year 2006, the NSF projects that the United States will have a shortfall of 675,000 science and engineering graduates, that there will be demands for 24,000 new engineering and science Ph.D.s each year but only 10,000 degrees awarded (many to foreign students who will return to their own countries), and that the situation probably is not much better in Europe or Japan.[2]

Another pressure necessitating more effective R&D is the modern competitive environment, in which the rapid and sustained introduction of high-quality, innovative, cost-effective new products has become the name of the game.

Companies that manufacture discrete objects such as consumer electronics, medical instrumentation, machine tools, process control instruments, and office equipment are feeling intense pressure to improve product quality and features, lower costs, and reduce the development time for new products. The loss of earnings for products whose development takes two years instead of one can be staggering. One could note the effect on General Motors' earnings by being late with "me-too" products in response to Ford's "European-design look" Taurus. Even if competitors have not already seized a leadership position because of the delay, the opportunity costs can still be great. Of about 500 chief executives surveyed recently by United Research, a large number named shortening product-development cycles as their first priority.[3]

All companies face the urgency of lead-time reduction. Many companies, particularly well-established ones, face the additional conflict of balancing the demands of supporting and expanding existing businesses with undertaking the original research that will produce major new products and processes within a 5–10 year period. Those companies include players in pharmaceuticals, advanced memory storage systems, intelligent robots, chemicals, aircraft propulsion, medical diagnostics, solar energy conversion, the next generation of office automation equipment, and countless other industries that demand technological innovation and excellence. Strategically correct R&D goals will pay off for these companies; strategically incorrect goals will waste scarce resources—and worse, irrecoverable time.

Our thesis is that senior business and corporate management must enter the era of third generation R&D management. In this era, corporate, business, and R&D managers work as partners to establish overall R&D strategies that are tightly linked with business and corporate strategies and vision and that focus on providing value to customers and shareholders in perpetuity. A shorthand characterization of third generation R&D management is shown in Figure 1-1. Descriptions of all three generations are developed in Chapter 3.

Clearly, if there is a disconnect between any of the functions in Figure 1-1 that drive success toward the company's strategic goal—that is, if corporate, business, and R&D management fail to act in partnership—there is diminished probability of success. The role of senior management is important, because only senior management has the authority to mobilize the resources to ensure the integration of all plans into one cohesive, mutually reinforcing plan. Only senior management can authorize the capital, marketing, manufacturing, sales, and executive support required to translate R&D results into enhanced competitive position and earnings.

It cannot be proved quantitatively, but a great deal of experience and most of the literature on the subject argue that senior management, especially in the United States, often does a bad job of thinking through these strategic connections. It is well-established business lore that many senior managers see their role in R&D planning as one of providing money, not providing the leadership and discipline demanded for excellence. A survey by the Industrial Research Institute reported that fewer than one-third of senior managers involve themselves even at the most rudimentary level of formal R&D project evaluation and selection.[4]

Lowell Steele, the former director of strategic planning for General Electric, asks: "How can the Japanese move so fast in introducing new products and responding to market dynamics? The answer clearly does not lie in access to or use of more advanced technology, because the United States still equals or leads the world in almost every field. The answer lies in management."[5]

Peter Drucker reinforced the point in a *Harvard Business Review* article: "The one great economic power to emerge in this century—Japan—has not been a technological pioneer in any area. Its ascendancy rests squarely on leadership in management."[6]

As Akio Morita, chairman and CEO of Sony, writes: "Technological management will be the key to success for companies anywhere in the world in the coming years.

Figure 1-1

Third generation R&D management—the indispensable components of success

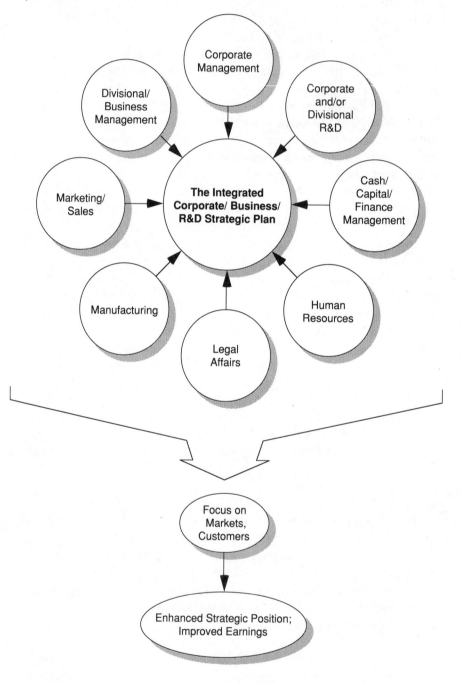

"We are quite advanced in it already. At Sony we have a monthly R&D report meeting attended by all top executives and heads of divisions."[7]

The Roots of Third Generation Management

The many roles of R&D have long been classified along a spectrum that emphasizes the cause-effect and time relationships of these interdependent responsibilities. However, the traditional classification system—from basic research to applied research, development, design, and finally technical services—hides the diversity of technology and strategic dynamics within each activity and the complexity of their interdependence.

Many companies prepare plans separately for each activity and relate between them only sequentially: "Once we are successful in research we will worry about development." "Only when we succeed with development need we consider our design approach." "We simply cannot plan production until design and engineering have come through." And so on.

Companies following such an approach—mistakenly evaluating their R&D on a sequential and piecemeal basis—are prone to fall into a large trap. The trap is strategic, albeit with operational implications.

This strategic trap is embarking on a project without first assessing the full consequences of its success. For instance, someone in R&D has an idea for a revolutionary process to make the common plastic polyvinyl chloride (PVC). He is assigned one associate and given six months to explore the idea and formulate a project proposal. He delivers on time at a total cost of $100,000, the bulk of the cost representing professional time. The proposal calls for a laboratory-scale two-year applied research program to test his hypothesis, at a total cost of $1 million, of which 25 percent would be out-of-pocket expenses.

The project is approved, and again the team delivers. At this point, a proposal is put forth to build a pilot plant and undertake the scaling-up work required to demonstrate the commercial viability of the process. The estimated cost is $10 million, of which 70 percent would be out-of-pocket expenses.

After a few months' deliberation, the proposal is given the green light. On completion of the pilot program, the engineering people are called in. They estimate that commercialization would involve scrapping the existing plant and building a new one, at a cost of $300 million.

At this point a horrified top management complains that had it known what would be involved, it never would have given the go-ahead in the first place. The economic potential of the industry does not warrant such an investment. The implication is that if management had considered the consequence of R&D success from the beginning, it might have refused to fund the project on sound strategic grounds. At the least, it would have revised the technological objectives of the program in ways that might have helped ensure both technological and business viability. An extreme example? Perhaps, but not rare. Planning failure of this magnitude may not be known in your company, but smaller examples of it probably are.

In addition to ensuring effective communication within the head office, the executives of that office must see to it that communication between R&D and all operating functions, such as marketing and manufacturing, is productive, mutually respected, and continuous. What happens when communication is poor can be seen in a food-machinery company that for years had differentiated itself from competitors by the speed of its filling machines and continued to focus R&D on increasing speed. Upon introducing its latest machine—which operated at double the speed of the previous generation—the company was astonished to find that customers wanted not increased speed but improved operating flexibility and machine reliability. Customers actually preferred to install two slower machines to increase throughput and flexibility, a fact that could have been discerned if effective communication had been established between marketing and its customer service representatives and R&D.

Some companies are still managing R&D in what we define as the first generation mode: they hire good people, provide them with the best facilities money can buy, have them work in a "creative"—possibly remote—setting, leave them alone, and hope they produce commercially viable results. This is more true of large, multidivisional companies than of smaller companies; it is also more true within the "R" than within the "D" part of the equation.

This construct can be called "the strategy of hope." Gary Hamel and C. K. Prahalad, in a *Harvard Business Review* article, described the Silicon Valley approach to innovation: "Put a few bright people in a dark room, pour in money, and hope."[8] The strategy of hope was a common R&D management method in large companies in the 1950s. The hope was that—given the right mix of brains, money, equipment, and time to pursue ideas—scientists and engineers, left alone, would concoct new products and processes that would translate into revenues, earnings, and market share.

Through the 1950s and the early 1960s, most industries enjoyed untapped technological potential, substantial growth, and healthy profits. Throughout those years, the strategy of hope produced results. But times have changed. Many once-revolutionary technologies—like the design and production of the chips at the technological heart of handheld calculators or microprocessor-controlled home appliances—are approaching their full potential. What once were innovative, cutting-edge products are now commodities. In industry after industry, demand growth has slowed or disappeared, and heightened competitive intensity has put severe pressure on profitability. Inevitably, the pressure has been extended to expectations of larger contributions from R&D.

Today companies are looking to technology and to their R&D organizations to help renew growth and profitability. They feel a need for more creativity, more effectiveness, and more efficiency in R&D, and they have effectively challenged the first generation strategy of hope.

The challenge has led top executives to recognize that the intuition and special insight characteristic of first generation R&D management are no longer sufficient, that they (the top executives) often possess insufficient insight and therefore insufficient intuition regarding their company's R&D. They tend to be distant from it in both mind and spirit. In the first generation mode, R&D was an overhead cost, a line item in the budget. Resources were allocated to R&D cost centers typically defined by discipline, rather than to discrete activities defined by their objectives. Results and progress were monitored on the basis of ritualistic descriptions of the work performed. First generation R&D lacked a strategic framework; future technologies were in the hands of the R&D function alone.

The past decade or two has seen the emergence of second generation R&D management practices within many companies—practices that are distinctly more systematic and more specifically attuned to business needs. Second generation R&D management recognizes the discrete—project—nature of research and development and seeks to quantify the cost and benefits of individual projects and to monitor progress against project objectives. But even in the second generation mode, corporations tend to manage R&D on a project-by-project basis, rather than managing the aggregate of all projects. Although each individual project may have merit, the collection, or portfolio, of projects may or may not be strategically adequate. Ten projects, each individually attractive but each focused on one business of several or one competitive thrust of several, probably will not constitute a well-balanced portfolio. Consequently, managers working in this mode find it difficult to establish priorities among projects within each business, across businesses, and for the corporation as a whole. In Chapter 3 we further examine this mode of management.

At the same time, some companies have begun to adopt what we call third generation management, which is both purposeful and strategic. In third generation R&D, general managers and R&D managers work as partners to share and pool their insights in deciding what to do, why, and when. In so doing, they take account of the needs of each business and of the corporation. They realistically assess costs, benefits, and risk/reward, and they balance these variables within a portfolio of R&D activity that best fulfills the purposes of the corporation as a whole.

Third generation management is not a mechanical model that allows managers to plug in variables and come up with decisions. Rather, it is a conceptual model that fosters the creation of productive working relationships and shared insights that allow competent managers from R&D and from the rest of the company to make the best judgments about what R&D to do and not do, now and in the medium- and longer-term future in a particular corporate environment.

Third generation management of R&D is not intrinsically new. The underlying concepts go back to the early days of industrial R&D. Indeed, as Lowell Steele points out in his historical account of R&D management, R&D managers and staff in the 1930s "attempted to identify the intersection of technical opportunity and business need or opportunity that would have the greatest leverage"; "worried about balance between short-term and long-term, and between focused and exploratory work"; and "felt an urgent need to demonstrate their worth through identifiable contributions to the success of the enterprise."[9]

The difference between the R&D management of the 1930s and today's third generation R&D management is discernible not in the attitudes or activities of the R&D manager but in the environment in which he operates. References to R&D management are inclusive of the communion of senior corporate and business managers and R&D managers. There is no escape from the role of corporate and business management in effective R&D. Today, R&D management must try to do what Steele says the R&D manager of the 1930s did, but within a larger, more complex, often multibusiness and multinational—or global—company and with many new sources of competition. Balancing the variables is far more difficult now than it was in the 1930s. Today, the spirit of communion between general manager and R&D manager that existed in the 1930s and the war years no longer comes naturally. Now it must be managed.

The Shift to Third Generation Is Demanding

More than ever, corporate executives and general business managers are troubled by the question: What are we getting for our investment in R&D? Underlying this question is business managers' pronounced feeling that they are spending much and that the return may not be commensurate with the spending. In the worst case, top management views its R&D function as a black box—the input is money, the activities within the box are not comprehensible, and the output is uncertain but never enough. "At present," Lowell Steele observes, "most CEOs cannot even get credible answers to the question, 'how are we doing in technology?' "[10]

A sense of lost opportunity is driving companies to seek ways to make R&D management more purposeful. Few have fully succeeded. A number of factors interact to make purposeful management of R&D particularly difficult.

The first, and in many ways the most difficult, obstacle to overcome is the gap between the worlds of R&D and the company's general management, two worlds with often disparate cultures and different outlooks. In many companies, business managers have a limited familiarity with technology and R&D. Most lack technical training—the springboards to top management are more likely to be marketing and finance than engineering or scientific research. Even when the chief executive does have a technical background, most of the senior managers do not; and regardless of the chief executive's background, the demands on scarce management time dictate that the chief executive cannot delve deeply into R&D matters.

Top managers are often concerned that any attempt to impose directive management on R&D might stifle creativity and "kill the goose that laid the golden egg." Even in small companies, where the CEO often has intimate understanding of R&D efforts, concern about striking the proper balance between creativity and directive management is common.

At the same time, many R&D managers find it difficult and frustrating to link the science and technologies they practice to the company's strategic business concerns.

Some companies have moved toward integrated business/R&D plans at the project level. Many, however, still struggle with the full transition to strategic integration for a complete business, across businesses, and for the corporation as a whole.

Even when the transition to project management has been established, the failure in crucial communication can be severe. It is illustrated in the case of Ingersoll-Rand, an American machinery and equipment company with sales of about $3 billion. The head of new business (new product) development for a division was charged with the responsibility to collapse the product-development cycle.

> He pondered the sorry development process, best seen as a succession of walls. Marketing would think up a product and throw it over the wall separating it from the engineering department. Engineering would work up a design and toss it over another wall to manufacturing, which would make the product and hurl it over the wall to sales. Those people would then try to sell it to customers who perhaps did not want it in the first place.
>
> Things, however, never flowed that smoothly. In practice, engineering would look at what had come flying over and say, "did some lunatic dream this up?" and whip it back to marketing. Later, it would thunder back in revised form. When it got heaved to manufacturing, the people there would commonly smirk, "the engineers have really been hitting the bottle." Back it would go. The point at which a product appeared was often fixed by when people's arms got too tired to throw anything more over the wall.[11]

If any more support for the critical role of management is needed, Jerome Wiesner, Institute Professor Emeritus and the former president of MIT, supplies it when he writes: "The major problem in both cases [the U.S. steel and automotive industries] was at the top. These two industries were plagued by leaders who lacked a vision of continued greatness for their companies or any appreciation of what science and technology could do for them."[12]

The aims of this book are to enhance the appreciation of industrial leaders for what science and technology can do for them and to develop their understanding of the purposeful and strategic management of R&D that drives profitable advances in science and technology.

Notes

1. Bruce S. Old, "Corporate Directors Should Rethink Technology," *Harvard Business Review* (January–February 1982), pp. 6–14.
2. "Barriers to Innovation in Industry—Opportunities for Public Policy Changes," National Science Foundation sponsored study by Arthur D. Little, Inc., and Industrial Research Institute (NSF C748 and C725).
3. "Response Time Is the Next Competitive Weapon," *Chief Executive* (November–December 1989), pp. 72–73.
4. Lowell W. Steele, "Selecting R&D Programs and Objectives," *Research & Technology Management,* vol. 31, no. 2 (March–April 1988), p. 17 ff.
5. *Ibid.*
6. Peter Drucker, "Management and the World's Work," *Harvard Business Review* (September–October 1988), p. 65.
7. Akio Morita, "Technological Management Will Be the Key to Success," *Research and Technology,* vol. 30, no. 2 (March–April 1987), p. 12.
8. Gary Hamel and C. K. Prahalad, "Strategy and Intent," *Harvard Business Review* (May–June 1989), p. 63.
9. Steele, "Selecting R&D Programs and Objectives."
10. Lowell W. Steele, *Managing Technology* (New York: McGraw-Hill, 1989), p. 1.
11. "How Strikeforce Beat the Clock," *New York Times,* March 25, 1990, sec. 3, p. 1.
12. Jerome B. Wiesner, "More R&D in the Right Places," *The MIT Report* (April 1988), p. 3.

Chapter 2

What Are: Technology? Research? Development?

Before proceeding, we must define what we mean by three key terms: technology, research, and development.

Technology is often confused with science and engineering on the one hand and with a product and its function on the other. To say that a company's technology is "computer science," "polymer physics," "chemical engineering," "mainframe computers," "engineering plastics," or "pressure vessels" is to define *technology* too broadly to be useful.

We view technology as the application of scientific and engineering knowledge to achieve a practical result. *Technology* is the process that enables a company to say, "We know how to apply science/engineering to . . . ," in a way that clarifies what the technology does for the business instead of just stating what the technology is. By this definition, science and engineering are embedded in the product or process by technology. This definition can be illustrated by several statements that identify the technologies involved in the automated teller machine (ATM) industry:

- The supplier of the plastic card must know how to apply science and engineering to select the plastic resins and plastic additives that make for a dimensionally stable card that does not warp with temperature variations (a materials technology).
- The same supplier must know how to process these materials to make the dimensionally stable card (a process technology).
- A component supplier must know how to design and make the reliable mechanical paper-handling device for the ATM (design and manufacturing technologies).
- The ATM supplier must know how to provide the software to integrate the operating system into the customer transactions network (an organized knowledge technology).
- The ATM supplier must know how to physically integrate the

13

ATM components into an operating system (a systems technology).

■ The ATM supplier must understand applications technologies: how the customer will use the operating system, what technical performance features are critical, and how the product economics compare with the alternatives available to the customer.

To the academician and those who work in research institutes, *research* means an orderly approach to the revelation of new knowledge about the universe. The objective of research is to advance knowledge and understanding, and the boundaries of the search are limitless.

Industrial research shares this quest for new knowledge, but its goals are ultimately far different from those of the academic researcher. In industry, the research goal is knowledge applicable to a company's business needs that will enable the company to participate in the forefront of new technology or lay the scientific foundation for the development of new products or processes—anything from a noncaloric fat substitute to a manufacturing process managed by intelligent computers instead of by humans.

Although there is no precise demarcation between the definitions of *research* and *development,* a broad distinction can be made. If the purpose of research is to develop new knowledge, the purpose of development is to apply scientific or engineering knowledge, to expand it, to connect the knowledge in one field—such as microcircuits—with that in other fields—such as the low-cost manufacturability of high-quality electronic materials. Development applies and connects those principles to develop reliable, high-quality, useful, manufacturable microcircuitry-based products. In the general case, development seeks to move product or process concepts through a series of definite stages to prove, refine, and ready them for commercial application.

In industrial R&D there is no hierarchy of importance in the contributions of "R" and "D." No company relies entirely on research for its technological success. In companies that undertake research, "R" must be translated by creative "D" into practical, profitable reality. Many companies conduct little or no research but rely for their success on the clever, creative development of the results of others' research.

Among widely recognized companies, IBM and Sony conduct substantial "R" and substantial "D." Apple Computer, by reputation, conducts little "R" but craftily applies the results of the world's "R" in exceptionally creative "D."

Three Basic Types of R&D

Given these definitions, there are three basic types of R&D: incremental, radical, and fundamental. Each has its own distinct characteristics and business purposes.

Incremental R&D: Small "r" and Big "D"

The goal of incremental R&D is small advances in technology, typically based on an established foundation of scientific and engineering knowledge. The task is therefore not the technically risky one of uncovering and applying new knowledge but the clever application of existing knowledge.

A typical example of incremental R&D is work on reducing manufacturing costs. Most manufacturing processes can be improved by a continuing series of small but important advances: energy conservation, computer-guided process control, better metallurgy for lower maintenance costs. Although each incremental improvement is small, in the aggregate they typically produce meaningful savings, often millions of dollars per year, that the company can use for an improved margin or for increased market share by more aggressive pricing. The small, incremental technical steps yield large strategic results.

Radical R&D: Large "R" and Often Large "D"

Radical R&D draws on a foundation of existing scientific and engineering knowledge that is insufficient alone to arrive at the desired practical result. The work undertakes the discovery of new knowledge with the explicit goal of applying that knowledge to a useful purpose. In the case of a new blood analyzer and its associated reagents, for example, research would have to devise highly specific blood component separations and analytical methods not yet known.

Progress toward this goal involves elements of discovery—that is, of learning things not already known. Discovery involves substantial technical risk, cost, and time. There is never certainty that R&D will get—in a practical, cost-effective way—all the technical success needed for commercial success. If market success demands, for example, the separation, characterization, and analysis of blood components at a certain level of accuracy and R&D cannot provide the accuracy for all of the components needed by the market, the project may be a commercial failure. Because of these inherent risks the business must see the potential of a substantial reward. Mitigating these negatives, however, is the fact that if R&D succeeds, the business will probably have know-how no competitor has, probably a protected position for many years, and the demonstration to customers of technological leadership—not a bad image for marketers to exploit.

Most radical R&D projects fail. If the business says "no" to them, it will be right 80 percent of the time. But the 20 percent about which the business will be wrong are the projects that would have provided the high-margin products or processes whose earnings would have distinguished the company from lesser competitors.

In radical R&D the risk is not always severe. Usually, projects of this kind begin as exploratory projects, or feasibility studies, intended to test the basic concepts on which the scientific foundation of the project rests. The exploratory phase usually involves only one or two or three researchers, and the cost is modest. Cost usually begins to soar when the work enters the development phase. But the decision to enter development occurs only after successful research has already sharply reduced uncertainty to levels acceptable to the business. Consciously managing radical R&D in this way is a means to reduce risk.

Fundamental R&D: Large "R" and No "D"

Fundamental R&D is a scientific/technological reach into the unknown. It has two principal goals: (1) to develop a depth of research competence in fields of potential future technology that the company is convinced—or at least persuaded—will have great strategic impact in the long term (8 to 15 years out) and (2) to prepare for future commercial exploitation of these fields.

Fundamental R&D offers some of the most painful strategic decisions a company's management must make. Should the company undertake it at all? Because it won't pay off for many years—if ever—management must decide whether to dilute earnings during its tenure and have the rewards accrue to the next generation of top management. There will no doubt be a host of uncertainties—scientific, competitive, social, and governmental—5 to 10 years or more from now. And even if management has the vision and the guts to consider fundamental research, in what fields does investing make sense?

The Strategic Role of R&D

Managing R&D strategically means first and foremost integrating R&D into technology and business strategy, then managing the R&D process, including its linkages broadly throughout the company, with the same dedication with which other critical pieces of the corporate structure are managed. In the proper strategic context, R&D should further the products that marketing and sales offer, the processes that manufacturing operates, and many of the investment decisions that management makes.

Industrial R&D has three major strategic purposes, as shown in Figure 2-1:

To defend, support, and expand existing business
To drive new business
To broaden and deepen a company's technological capabilities

Existing business support includes modifying products to improve customer acceptance or adapting them to different market standards or regulations, using different or new raw materials or improvements in manufacturing processes, and dealing with nondiscretionary activities such as safety considerations and environmental compliance. Business support also includes developing new products and manufacturing processes to improve competitive position within the existing business structure.

Figure 2-1

The strategic purposes of R&D

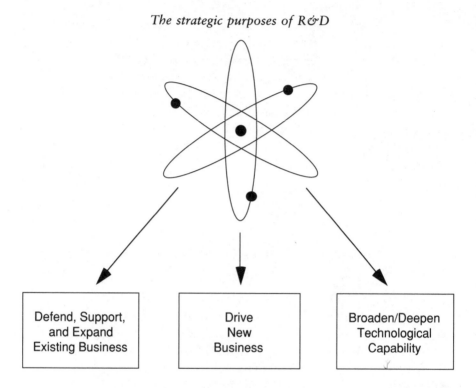

Defend, Support, and Expand Existing Business	Drive New Business	Broaden/Deepen Technological Capability

Driving new business involves providing opportunities for new businesses using existing or new technologies. The new businesses may be new for the company or new to the world. Similarly, the new technologies may be new to the world or new only to the company, as might be the case with licensed-in technologies.

Broadening and deepening technological capabilities may concern existing or new business, depending on the perceived opportunity and the company's competitive position.

The R&D, and strategic, mission of a company typically changes as a function of the maturity of the industry in which the company competes. As shown in Figure 2-2, the business mission of R&D at the embryonic stage of the industry life cycle is to help launch the new business and establish position by demonstrating the validity of the product concept in one or more applications and by establishing the viability of the manufacturing process. The mission may also include doing what is needed to establish and defend the company's intellectual property.

Figure 2-2

The mission of R&D and the industry cycle

EMBRYONIC	GROWTH	MATURE	AGING

The R&D Mission

Launch new business
Establish competitive position

Grow new business
Improve competitive position

Sustain competitive position

Rejuvenate?

Renew?

Abandon?

→ Industry Maturity

Figure 2-3

The R&D strategy cycle is an iterative and continual process

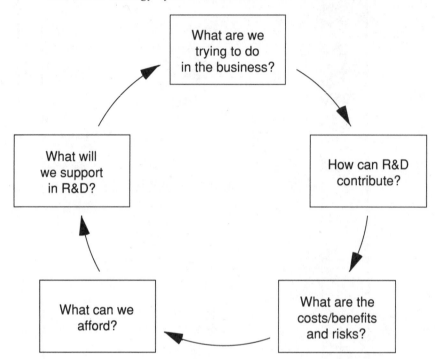

During the growth stage, the purpose of R&D is to help grow the business and improve or sustain its competitive position by extending the range of products and applications or by enlarging the application potential of existing products through improved features or reduced cost.

When the industry becomes mature, the strategic role of R&D usually shifts to one of defending competitive position by extending the differentiation potential of products or focusing on cost reduction. Management may decide to rejuvenate the business, and this may also become an R&D responsibility.

In an aging industry, the classical role of R&D has been cost reduction and providing the customer support necessary to safeguard profitability. Strategically, perhaps a better R&D thrust in the aging phase is to renew the products or technology of manufacturing and drive competitors out of business rather than be driven out.

To this point, we have established the imperatives of R&D for the 1990s and beyond. We have established the historical roots of the widely prevalent shortcomings in much of current R&D planning. We have established common definitions of *technology, research,* and *development.* We have emphasized the critical need for unending partnership between R&D and all major business functions, including top management, in the iterative R&D strategy cycle, illustrated in simplified form in Figure 2-3.

In the remainder of this book, we extend the analysis of the competitive importance of R&D and, most particularly, of the critical role of the business/R&D partnership in ensuring the profitability of R&D for companies in competitive environments.

In the next chapter, we provide detailed characterizations of the three generations of R&D management. Then we describe planning principles that equip business and R&D executives to play their vital roles in integrating business and R&D strategies and the operational principles that make that process work. Throughout the book we continually refer to a fictitious composite company that we call Intercontinental. We show how Intercontinental, with powerful executive leadership, is able to propel itself from a position between first and second generation R&D management to a position firmly in the third generation.

Chapter 3

A Framework for Purposeful R&D Management

The purposeful management of R&D is a complex and delicate balancing act. General management wants R&D to serve multiple purposes: supporting existing businesses, helping launch new businesses, and deepening or broadening the company's technological capabilities. General management wants R&D to produce results as quickly as possible but is willing to wait for radical results—as long as the potential reward is commensurate with the wait and the competition does not get there first. General management is willing to assume higher risk in some circumstances or in some businesses more than in others, and some individual managers are willing to take larger risks than others. A company prefers high rewards when they are available but always expects rewards to be commensurate with the risks involved. Furthermore, the resources that management is willing to make available to R&D are always limited—and the correct strategic balance must be struck with that ever-present constraint. The inevitable tensions between management wants and resource constraints are outlined in Figure 3-1.

To respond to these various management wants, R&D engages in types of work characterized by different technological uncertainties and differing time frames. The uncertainties and time frames depend on the nature of the technological weapons chosen to fight the particular battle—the maturity of the technologies involved and the degree to which they are mastered by the company. This in turn depends on the quality and quantity of the resources R&D can muster when it needs them. However, resource flexibility in R&D is inherently limited in the short term by the type and quantity of skills available within the company. In some companies resource flexibility is also limited by the lack of mobility of people resources and funds across organizational boundaries. The latter problem is seen particularly in companies that have substantially distributed their R&D to their individual businesses. Flexibility is further limited in most companies by policies that favor relying on internal resources rather

23

Figure 3-1

Corporate/R&D tensions

Management Wants	Resource Constraints
Favorable risk/reward situations	Limited finances
Timely results	Limited time
Results that serve business purposes	Limited talent
	Basic uncertainty of outcomes

than drawing on external skills—the bias toward "making" rather than "buying."

Purposeful management of R&D runs counter to the mindset developed and ways of managing acquired over decades of industrial growth and opportunity during which industrial R&D was prosecuted in user-friendly environments characterized by plenty of opportunities and nearly boundless resources. During the Second World War, the national strategic imperatives of many countries were such that money was no object. Since the end of the war, and until recently, money continued to be generally available throughout the industrialized world for both military-industrial and industrial-commercial R&D. The first was often justified, partly at least, in terms of national defense—particularly in the United States, where major successes in electronics, computer technology, and aviation were made.

In industrial R&D, the environment from the 1930s through the 1950s was one of boundless opportunity. There was a lot of technology, a lot of potential, and a lot of money; seemingly everywhere a researcher or a company dropped a hook, there were fish. In the United States, the government market for the results of industrial R&D was vast; in Japan, the government provided direct support to industrial research and development. Governments in all the industrially advanced nations were liberal in their support of academic research.

By the late 1960s and into the 1980s, the situation had changed dramatically: vast tracts of R&D waters had been overfished, competition had intensified, and profits had been compressed. All of this, and the call for resources to meet the challenges of increasing globalization, meant that companies had to be more careful about how they used the cash flows they generated. Governments also had begun to feel the pinch as the demands on their national budgets mounted from all sides. Led by the United States, Western nations have become more selective in their support of military and commercial R&D and have begun to shift onto industry part of the burden of funding academic research.

The net result is that even the managers of technology and R&D-driven companies in the West are having to struggle to get more out of less—or the same—investment in R&D. The magnitude of the challenge for many of today's managers is all the more daunting because they have to deal with the complexity of strategically diverse activities resulting from organic growth; from geographic, business, and technological diversification; and from mergers and acquisitions.

Some companies have responded better and more rapidly to these changes than others. As we look on today's industrial scene, we see three generations of R&D (and technology) management in practice. The rest of this chapter describes in detail the salient characteristics of each generation. Subsequent chapters describe the practice of third generation management.

Recognizing which generations of R&D management are practiced in your company provides a foundation for change, when change is appropriate. How do you distinguish among them? You recognize them by their distinguishing traits: by the R&D management philosophy in place, by the way in which R&D is organized, by the way R&D/technology strategy is formulated, by how R&D is funded and how resources are allocated to R&D, by how R&D targets are selected and R&D priorities are set, and by the way R&D results and progress are measured and evaluated.

For each generation, we describe the management and strategic context in place, the operating principles in use, and the differences in management practices and systems used with the different types of R&D.

First Generation Management of R&D

First generation management of R&D is a holdover from the good old days of the 1950s and early 1960s. It is characterized by the lack of a strategic framework for the management of technology and R&D. This year's budget provides the total framework for R&D. General management possesses scant insight and provides little guidance. The company's future technology is decided largely by R&D alone.

The operational context can be described as fatalistic. R&D is an overhead cost, a line item in the general manager's budget. General management participates little in defining programs or projects; funds are allocated to cost centers; cost control is at aggregate levels. There is minimum evaluation of the R&D results other than by those involved in R&D. There is little communication from R&D other than to say, "Everything is going fine." There is only a modest sense of urgency: "Things are ready when they are ready." The communication and cooperation breakdown between R&D and the businesses is clear, and especially severe in radical and fundamental R&D.

These classic examples of managementspeak versus researchspeak characterize the "we/they" dialogue about R&D that still exists in many companies:[1]

- Business people believe that "R&D does not understand business," and researchers believe that "targeting stifles motivation."
- Business people think "researchers are uncontrollable," and researchers think that "administration smothers creativity."
- To the business mangers' complaints that "results are always 'just around the corner,' " the researchers retort that "breakthroughs cannot be forecast."

The Management and Strategic Context

In first generation management, the management philosophy is characterized by failures of confidence in the relationship between general business management and R&D management.

The intuitions of R&D managers predominate. They decide the *what, when, by whom,* and *why* of fundamental R&D in isolation from the broad business context. General management often remains aloof and sometimes does not even know that fundamental research is being carried out at all, let alone what it costs. Work is done "under the table" for fear that if general management finds out, the research will be discontinued.

In first generation management, the philosophy for radical R&D is analogous to a courtroom where R&D is the advocate and general management is the prosecutor. However, there is no judge, so the two parties enter into plea bargaining. R&D management proposes the *what* and the *why* and gives an indication of the *when* and *how much* but makes only loose commitments regarding timing and total cost. General management can only decide whether it is willing to approve next year's budget.

In the world of incremental R&D, the R&D manager often does the bidding of general and functional managers from areas such as marketing and production. Functional managers decide the *what, when, why,* and *how much* to spend, leaving R&D management to figure out the *how* and *by whom.* Companies practicing first generation management of their incremental R&D have much to gain by carefully reviewing all incremental R&D work being done to, for example, improve product quality or to reduce production costs and then evaluating whether the benefits are worth the costs. The conventional wisdom is that such work is "always good for you." This truism may obscure the real reason the work is being done—*momentum turned to inertia.* The work was started because it was needed; it was continued because it did some good; it is maintained because "we have always done it."

In first generation management, R&D is typically organized into cost centers by scientific or engineering discipline. Much R&D is centralized at the corporate or divisional level, and incremental R&D is distributed to the business units. Incremental R&D is often grouped first into activity centers such as clinical development in pharmaceuticals, field development in pesticides, design and prototype development in machinery companies, "bread-boarding" in electronics, and piloting in chemicals. Then it is further broken down by technological discipline or expertise center—clinical medicine, biology, rotary equipment, software development, corrosion, and so on.

Project management—meaning a discrete set of activities with a specific objective, a resource plan, a time frame, and a budget—is not explicitly recognized in first generation management. Responsibility for activities is assigned to one line manager or another in the hierarchical R&D organization. In such companies, the matrix-type organization, with a project manager as a full partner, is avoided as an unnecessary complication and an incursion into the realm of line management. As a result, responsibility for achieving the R&D objective is obfuscated as it is handed over from one line manager to another—for example, from an electronic design laboratory to the engineering department. As responsibility is passed from one department to another, advancing the R&D objective may get unequal attention. In either case, continuity and accountability are elusive.

The R&D strategy problem in first generation management is rooted in the difficulty of defining technology in ways that both technologists and business managers understand and feel comfortable with. General managers working in a first generation mode tend to see technology in terms of scientific and engineering disciplines—at the incremental end, mostly in terms of what a technology is and much less in terms of what it does for the business. In such companies, the importance of technology is judged from the perspective of the technologist. Novelty is one major consideration; the expertise of veteran technologists is another.

Technological uncertainty is taken as an uncontrollable given that will decline over time. But technological uncertainty is difficult to assess. Business and market uncertainties are subjects for the business and marketing managers to worry about, and only when the work is sufficiently advanced do technological and business uncertainties merge. No wonder then that the conventional wisdom is to "develop the technology first and link it to the business later," or to "let the general and functional managers worry about the business aspects and leave technology to the technologists," much as one might suggest leaving war to the generals. The danger in the approach is clear. Polaroid, for example, came out with a new instant movie-camera film system just as videocassette cameras were coming on the market.

Operating Principles

In first generation management, the funding of R&D—the aggregate levels of expenditure and where in the corporation they are accounted for—is at the discretion of general management even though the CEO and general managers at the division and business levels typically have limited insight into the company's future technological needs on which to base funding decisions. R&D expenditure is merely a line item in the budget. Furthermore, where the funds are accounted for is often a matter of affordability, convenience, or both, giving rise to accusations of "robbing Peter to pay Paul."

R&D resource allocation, in contrast, is at the discretion of R&D; only the R&D managers at various levels know how the funds are expended. R&D budgeting is done by means of a top-down cascade, and each level defines how it will spend the part of the budget that falls within its direct control. There is little upward visibility. More often than not, availability influences how resources are used; business objectives and needs have little influence in the short and medium term on the resource configuration.

Scientists, engineers, and R&D managers working in radical or fundamental R&D in the first generation mode view targeting, milestones, and dates as the imposition of rigid linear logic on a process of idea generation and exploration that thrives on creativity, intuition, and spatial reasoning. They cite serendipitous discoveries of immeasurable corporate and human benefit. Aspartame, for example, was discovered when James Schlatter of G. D. Searle, while working on something other than an artificial sweetener, licked his finger and found that what he was working on was sweet; and a 3M researcher, by intelligent accident, discovered Scotchguard fabric protector.[2]

There is no denying the power of creativity, intuition, and spatial reasoning, or their untold benefits. The problem for companies using the first generation approach, however, is that later, when R&D yields results, the linkage between those results and the business' needs is or may be haphazard. General management is uncertain how to influence the situation. Furthermore, if targeting is not even acknowledged as useful, priority setting is not even considered.

Targeting and priority setting are more acceptable in incremental R&D because technological uncertainty is not a significant factor and the time frame is typically more immediate. The business targets for incremental R&D are selected by the general and functional managers, and R&D objectives and resources are subsequently defined by R&D. A first attempt is made to match the two during the annual budget cycle, but the real trade-offs between needs and resources are made during the course of the year; priority setting is operational, not strategic.

Measuring results, and thus evaluating R&D progress, tends to be ritualistic and perfunctory in the first generation. To begin with, result expectations are not defined rigorously from the outset. "We seek a novel chemical entity," "we are aiming at an innovative new widget," or "we want a lower-cost manufacturing process" are not precise enough definitions of results against which to evaluate success or progress.

In these circumstances, progress reviews tend to focus on scientific and technological problems and how they might be resolved. In fundamental and radical R&D, activities are peer-reviewed periodically, typically every six months or one year; and the emphasis is on technological achievements since the last review, in light of the effort expended and the obstacles still to be overcome. Progress and results of incremental R&D are reviewed in terms of what has been done during the past three or six months, whether what was done was on time, and whether the cost centers involved were on budget. Figure 3-2 highlights the characteristics of first generation management.

Second Generation Management of R&D

Second generation R&D management is a transition state between the intuitive and the purposeful styles of management. It is practiced by companies that recognize the reinforcing interrelationship among organizational functions and seek to introduce greater order into their management.

Second generation management provides the beginnings of a strategic framework for R&D at the project level and seeks to enhance communications between business and R&D management by making business or the corporation the "external customer" for R&D practitioners alongside—and equally as important as—the "internal customer," R&D management. Long-range plans and annual budgets in these companies recognize projects as distinct and discrete activities. Management also recognizes explicitly the differences among the strategically distinct types of R&D and tries to set a course to differentiate them in strategic and operating policies.

Second generation management is most distinctly differentiated from the first generation by business and R&D management's cooperation in the joint consideration of individual projects—projects' cost over their lifetimes, their impact on the businesses, their uncertainties, their management, and their execution.

For individual projects, the results can be splendid. But the consideration of and decisions about projects on a project-by-project basis, however beneficial for each individual project, still omits the strategic dimension dealt with in third generation management: the interrelationships among projects within a business, across businesses, and for the corporation as a whole.

The purposeful management of R&D at the business and corpo-

Figure 3-2

The characteristics of first generation R&D management (the intuitive mode)

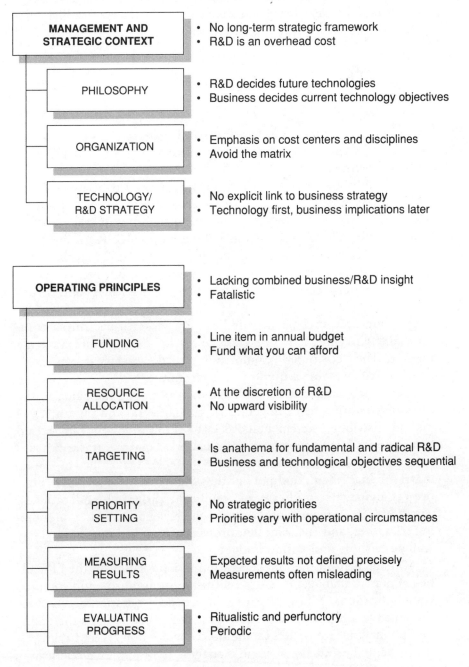

MANAGEMENT AND STRATEGIC CONTEXT	• No long-term strategic framework • R&D is an overhead cost
PHILOSOPHY	• R&D decides future technologies • Business decides current technology objectives
ORGANIZATION	• Emphasis on cost centers and disciplines • Avoid the matrix
TECHNOLOGY/ R&D STRATEGY	• No explicit link to business strategy • Technology first, business implications later

OPERATING PRINCIPLES	• Lacking combined business/R&D insight • Fatalistic
FUNDING	• Line item in annual budget • Fund what you can afford
RESOURCE ALLOCATION	• At the discretion of R&D • No upward visibility
TARGETING	• Is anathema for fundamental and radical R&D • Business and technological objectives sequential
PRIORITY SETTING	• No strategic priorities • Priorities vary with operational circumstances
MEASURING RESULTS	• Expected results not defined precisely • Measurements often misleading
EVALUATING PROGRESS	• Ritualistic and perfunctory • Periodic

rate (i.e., multibusiness) level is still missing. The portfolio concept remains absent. The spirit of partnership between general and R&D management continues to be project focused. Even though the managerial and strategic principles of project evaluation in a strategic context may be clear for senior managers, they do not readily penetrate the company's operational levels.

The Management and Strategic Context

The management philosophy in the second generation is characterized by a relationship in which general management seeks to balance the advocacy and championship of R&D against strategic goals without destroying motivation.

By establishing a supplier/customer relationship between R&D and business managers, business managers hope to become "bottom-line responsible" for what they choose to spend on R&D and thus more cost/benefit conscious and willing to involve R&D management to a greater extent in cost/benefit assessment. They also hope to make R&D managers work hard to demonstrate their relevance and to be more responsive to the needs of their business and corporate clients.

Although the management philosophy seeks to institute a commercial environment, it does not go so far as to install an open market. The "customer" cannot buy outside services if equivalent services are available within the corporation.

Like management in the first generation mode, managing in the second generation tends to centralize fundamental and radical R&D and to distribute incremental R&D to the businesses. But second generation R&D management has a major advantage: it clarifies and acts on the discrete, project nature of R&D, makes active use of matrix management, and puts professionally trained or experienced project managers in charge of significant programs and projects. These project managers are assigned the tasks of planning, mobilizing resources, and ensuring that projects are carried out on target as well as on time and within budget.

Management in the first generation mode focuses on the difficulties of matrix management—the diffusion of authority and complex communications. Management in the second generation accentuates the positive and adopts a proactive attitude. It recognizes the multidisciplinary nature of R&D, the need for continuity, and the need for dedicated professionalism in managing the complex relationships called for by most R&D projects of any size. The project manager is responsible for what is to be done, when, and at what cost. The line (or resource) managers are responsible for whom to assign to the team and for the quality of the output.

Second generation R&D management attempts to link R&D and technology to the needs of the business on a project-by-project basis. It allows R&D to challenge the appropriateness of business objectives and proactively to suggest how R&D and technology can constructively interact to produce a business plan, the quality of which neither alone could construct.

Still, it formulates R&D plans on a project-by-project basis, separately and independently for each business and for the corporation. The process fails to deal adequately with activities not directly related to existing businesses but important on a corporate level. The process is unable to optimize R&D resources for the businesses or for the corporation as a whole. The process offers no mechanism for deciding between, say, allocating a sum of resources to a cost-reduction project in business A or allocating the same sum to the development of a new product in business B, even though the benefits to the corporation may be significantly greater in one case than in the other.

Operating Principles

General funding parameters for fundamental research are established at a level the company feels it can afford, typically a largely arbitrary percentage of the R&D budget. These funds are provided centrally, by the corporation or the division.

Funding for radical R&D is often shared by the business and the division or the corporation in order to share risks. Funding levels are determined by the needs of existing businesses and those of new businesses and technologies important to the corporation, after assessment by the divisional or corporate staff responsible for new business and technology.

Funding of incremental R&D is typically through the business. The level is negotiated between business managers and their R&D counterparts, usually in the context of the annual budget.

Resource allocation and priority setting also vary across the R&D spectrum. Corporate central R&D management, where it exists, allocates resources and sets priorities for fundamental R&D. Resources for radical and incremental R&D projects are allocated and priorities are set through joint decisions by customers and suppliers. However, the make-or-buy decision is usually left to R&D managers, who base their choice on how flexible or inflexible their internal resources are and what work can be accommodated internally.

Management in the second generation usually tries to measure the results of R&D by using quantitative approaches, such as net present value, return on investment (ROI), and payout measures, for each project of significant size. General managers often find it hard to quantify the benefits early in the life of projects, before the technological uncertainties have been dealt with. Their quantitative characterizations are usually barren, less for lack of competence than for lack of discipline.

Often this management runs into a market intelligence gap. The marketing people say, "If you can tell us what you expect to achieve, we can tell you what the market might be." The R&D people say, "If you can tell us what the market will value in five years, we will be in a better position to give the market what it wants." The gap frustrates everyone. Marketing people generally have little or no idea what the market needs will be five years hence; they are paid to worry about the market this quarter, this year, and perhaps next year. The R&D people, on the other hand, usually have little direct access to market information; they are paid to do R&D.

As R&D work advances and the time to commercialization shortens, the market intelligence gap gradually closes, and management finds it can begin measuring results in terms that everyone feels comfortable with: cost, benefits, time, and the like. But early in the life of radical projects, management is reduced to measuring progress mainly against technological milestones.

Second generation management finds quantitative approaches to measurement even more daunting when it comes to fundamental research. The time frame to results is even longer, the uncertainties greater; and early on the benefits can be described only in the broadest of technological and business terms. Even the project's costs are difficult to estimate beyond the immediate future, since the project could be discontinued at any time and what may need to be done tomorrow is a function of today's results.[3]

Companies working in the first generation are fatalistic in their attitude toward evaluating progress. Their counterparts working in the second generation worry about how to reach decisions to accelerate or decelerate an effort and when abandoning an effort would be appropriate. They establish formalized peer-review systems that involve the best talent within the company and the best external talent they can find.

R&D managers communicate the results of these progress reviews regularly to their customers. However, as is often the case in commercial relationships, the vested interests of each side differ; the result is difficulties in deciding what to do when projects do not progress satisfactorily. A spirit of partnership is clearly still missing.

Figure 3-3 shows the salient characteristics of second generation management.

Third Generation Management of R&D

Third generation management seeks to create across business units, across divisions, and across the corporation a strategically balanced portfolio of R&D formulated jointly in a spirit of partnership between general managers and R&D managers.

R&D seeks to respond to the needs of existing businesses and to the additional needs of the corporation while at the same time contributing to the identification and exploitation of technological opportunities in existing and new businesses. General management in the third generation mode institutes a strategic and operational partnership between R&D and the other vital functions in which R&D challenges and helps define the company's real technological needs, both today and tomorrow, in addition to helping meet those needs. What appear to be examples of third generation management practices and successes can be found in IBM's development of the Proprinter[4] and Merck's introduction of several major new pharmaceuticals in a very short span of time. Is it a coincidence that Merck's CEO, Roy Vagelos, is a Ph.D./M.D. who came out of Merck's R&D labs?

Management and Strategic Context

How does third generation management differ from first and second generation management?

In management philosophy, third generation management creates a spirit of partnership and mutual trust between general and R&D managers. They jointly explore, assess, and decide the *what, when, why,* and *how much* of R&D.

Although general and functional business managers may not con-

Figure 3-3

*The characteristics of second generation R&D management (the systematic
mode)*

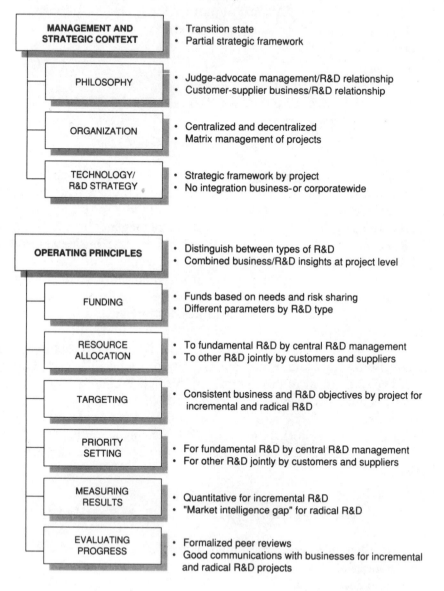

tribute insight into the *how* and *by whom* questions (particularly when they have no technological education or R&D experience), R&D managers in companies employing third generation management find it useful to inform their colleagues on these topics as a means of motivating their moral support. The partners recognize that, although each has a unique contribution to make to the managing of R&D, bringing the different perspectives together when preparing and making important decisions enhances the quality of these decisions.

Furthermore, companies working in the third generation take a holistic view of the full range of their R&D activities. On the one hand, they recognize the different strategic dynamics and the different sources and levels of uncertainty along the spectrum; on the other, they find it immensely valuable to understand and take into account the interrelationships among the activities concerned.

Companies working in the third generation seek to organize their R&D in a way that breaks the isolation of R&D from the rest of the company, in order to promote the spirit of partnership between R&D managers and their general or functional management counterparts. By concentrating scarce resources and rare skills, these companies organize to promote sharing where it matters. They exploit technological synergies by integrating their R&D and technology plans across businesses and across the corporation by coordinating plan execution and by sharing experiences and information between distributed centers. They design their communication networks to ensure a continuum across the R&D spectrum and forward to the market. They believe in the matrix as a powerful way of managing R&D, and they seek to make their project managers full partners with their R&D line-manager counterparts.[5] These companies work to formulate integrated corporate/business/R&D/technology strategies that take account of synergies and trade-offs between projects across businesses and corporate programs, particularly when technologies are shared by different parts of the corporation.

Such companies select targets by setting their fundamental research in a business context, confident that providing researchers with a sense of business purpose is a motivating factor and need not be inimical to creativity. They ask themselves questions such as these:

- How relevant and important to the company would the successful completion of program A be within the X years it might take?
- Do we have the critical mass of resources required? Are they in-house or available externally?

- Given their relative importance, likely time frames, and resource availability, should we proceed with all the programs
  proposed or only with some?
- Which programs should get priority?

Operating Principles

Third generation management (see Figure 3-4) establishes funding
levels for the short-, medium-, and long-term needs of the businesses
and the corporation. It seeks to afford what they need, rather than
simply funding what they think they can afford. Funding policies are
flexible.

If there is strategic space for R&D on emerging and young technologies, third generation management provides it at the corporate
and divisional levels. Speculative technologies are typically funded
at the corporate level when the risk is high enough to cause a business
unit to shy away from strategically desirable investment.

With incremental R&D, management encourages customers
within the company and their internal suppliers to test regularly the
charges they respectively receive and make against market rates for
similar work. When management is smart, it also periodically "zero-
bases" its incremental R&D and technical service budgets.

Companies operating in the era of third generation management
of R&D have a resource-allocation principle for radical R&D that
requires a strategic balancing between priority projects and technologies across business and corporate needs and opportunities.
They allocate resources to fundamental research on the basis of a
combination of technological merit, business relevance, and critical-
mass considerations. They do not shy away from conducting trade-
offs across businesses and among types of R&D.

For example, an incremental R&D project to improve process
efficiency in the short term in business A may be more or less worthy
than a radical R&D project to bring out a new product in the mid
term in business B. Third generation management takes a corporate
perspective. It assesses not only the direct rewards of each project
but the "springboard potential" to its businesses and to the corporation in the form of "step-out" potential, technological synergy, and
knowledge buildup. It assesses not only the strategic importance of
each project to its business but also the strategic importance of the
business to the corporation. It also assesses the nature of the skills
and resources needed and their relative availability or scarcity. Only
then does third generation management decide whether to choose

Figure 3-4

The characteristics of third generation R&D management (strategic and purposeful)

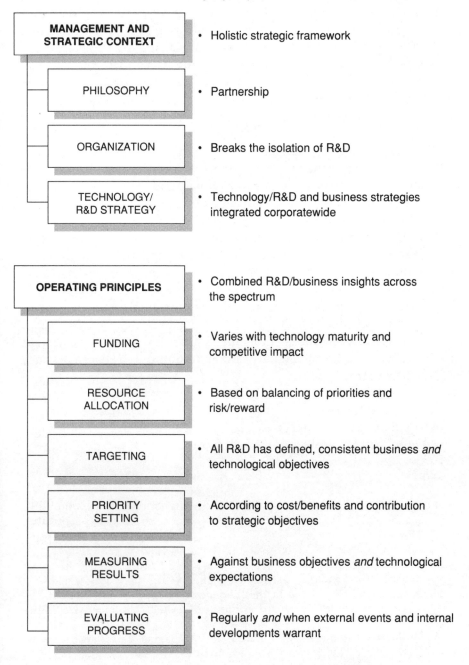

between projects or to accommodate both projects by increasing resources.

Finally, it works hard to maintain flexibility in internal resources. It does this by encouraging the use of multidisciplinary approaches, by making maximum use of external resources, and by always considering the "buy" alternative before investing to "make" internally.

It sets priorities regularly, for both radical and incremental R&D, between projects and technologies, according to their cost/benefits and contributions to business and corporate objectives, by their time frames, and by associated risks—all on a corporate portfolio basis. It also reassesses priorities whenever external events or internal developments warrant.

In the third generation, guidelines for measuring results and progress are rooted in the principle of management by objectives, which companies operating in this generational mode employ throughout their various R&D types by always examining the business implications of their own as well as external technological developments. The desired technological results are specified at the outset in light of business objectives. Progress is reviewed and results to date are reevaluated against expectations whenever significant external technological or business events warrant such review—not only in light of internal project developments and certainly not simply on an arbitrary time schedule.

Does this strike you as "utopian?" It isn't. It requires management will, intelligence, and commitment, and not more. Its characteristics are elementary.

In the next chapters, through the experience of an operating division of the Intercontinental Company, Inc., a composite example, we examine closely and illustrate how third generation R&D management can be applied in the real world.

Notes

1. David Gobeli and Daniel Brown, "Analyzing Product Innovation," *Research & Technology Management,* vol. 30, no. 4 (July–September 1987), p. 25.
2. Kenneth Labich, "The Innovators," *Fortune,* June 8, 1988, p. 56.
3. Thomas Lee, John C. Fisher, and Timothy S. Yan, "Is Your R&D on Track?" *Harvard Business Review* (January–February 1986), p. 34.
4. Ralph E. Gomory, "From the 'Ladder of Science' to the Product Development Cycle," *Harvard Business Review* (November–December 1989), p. 103.
5. William E. Sounder, "Stimulating and Managing Ideas," *Research & Technology Management,* vol. 30, no. 3 (May–June 1987), p. 13.

Chapter 4

Top Management and R&D

The new chief executive officer of Intercontinental Company, Inc., is fond of quoting Von Clausewitz' book *On War*: "Tactics are the use of forces to win an engagement. Strategy is the use of engagements to achieve the objectives of a war."[1]

Like all quotations that survive the decades, Von Clausewitz' continues to be cited because it combines profound insight and economy of expression with relevance far beyond that of its original intent. Its relevance here is apt: In the 1990s and beyond there will be no effective large-scale commercial enterprise that has not defined—and with great insight—the objective of its "war," the engagements it will seek, the correct deployment of its forces in the engagements in which it can succeed, and the avoidance of those in which it cannot.

The relevance of these remarks to effective R&D in the corporation of the future is complete and profound. It begins with the responsibility of corporate leadership to define the objective of its war and to provide the strategic vision, the resources, and then the concrete objectives whose attainment will satisfy that vision.

General managers, including the CEO but excluding managers with earlier incarnations in R&D, are often poorly prepared in experience, personality, and culture to establish and lead R&D for maximum return. Although CEOs accept risk, which is more or less quantifiable, many are temperamentally and culturally uncomfortable dealing with what they perceive as uncertainty in R&D. They see occasional successful results from R&D—a new product or a cost reduction. But they also know, from many sources, of multiple failures.

Many tend to regard R&D as a black box or ivory tower only loosely connected to the rest of the enterprise. The input to the black box is money. By mysterious workings within, the money either produces good results or does not. To many CEOs, R&D is the slot machine of the corporation. They feel almost helpless to influence the output. Because it is in their nature to control, to manage, to cause results to happen, this helpless feeling often leads the CEO to a sense of frustration, which in turn leads to tension, suspicion, distrust, and sometimes anger. And these can lead to arbitrary and ill-conceived action simply because a CEO feels "something" must be done.

The CEO is accustomed to rigor in much of his most important work. A CEO deals with manufacturing costs, which are precisely measurable and amenable to forecast; sales reports, which are quantitative; and sales forecasts, which are typically accurate in the short term—say, one year—to plus or minus 5 or 10 percent. A CEO deals with numbers and employee costs, which are knowable precisely, and with finance people and bankers who speak the language of numbers.

But R&D is different. There the CEO deals with costs rigorously, but not with output. He hears promises, excuses, delays, and assurances that the answer is "just around the corner," and language that is only partly understandable. He hears no rigor. Temperamentally uncomfortable with ambiguity and lack of quantitative information, the CEO may be frustrated, not surprisingly.

The new CEO of Intercontinental knows his general business managers and learns more about them every day but does not have much contact with his corporate R&D and business R&D managers. He has little personal technical background, and his sense of the place of R&D and technology in business success is more intuitive than detailed. He has spent most of his career in the financial services industry. His corporate vice president of technology—whom he refers to as the chief technology officer (CTO), has been with the company only six months but has a long and distinguished career at other companies.

Intercontinental is a company with five operating divisions in several industries. Figure 4-1 shows the business focus and annual sales of each division. The CEO begins his new role by reviewing the current conditions of the businesses and their plans, as well as the corporation's plans. Because he wants to get to know his people, the quality of their thinking, and the incisiveness and completeness of their planning, he does not suggest a structure for the reviews. He leaves to each of his five presidents and to his vice president of corporate planning the decision about the people to involve in presenting the material for review. Not wanting his reactions during the reviews to bias the structure, content, or participation of the

Figure 4-1

The Intercontinental Company, Inc.

Operating Divisions	Principal Business	Annual Sales
Haber Food Ingredients	Ingredients to the processed food industry	$700 MM
Medelectronics	Blood analyzers and reagents	510
Mason Seed	Hybrid corn and soybean seed	320
Microswitch	Ultra-fast switching devices	660
Home Easy Appliances	Small, upscale home appliances	1,890
	TOTAL	$4,080 MM

presenters, he resolves to participate by expressing keen interest and by asking questions only for clarification.

He can digest the content of an annual and projected five-year budget almost at a glance. Unlike budgets in his previous experience, each of the five divisional budgets has a line item for R&D, ranging in size from about 1 percent to about 9 percent of annual sales, the latter percentage being an absolute value greater than Intercontinental's annual pretax earnings. Moreover, the corporation as a whole has a separate R&D budget, called "Central Research," of about $40 million, altogether mysterious to him and startling when seen in the context of the $80 million in total dividends paid to stockholders the preceding year. R&D for the corporation exceeds $200 million, roughly two-thirds of the company's operating earnings of $320 million, daunting indeed.

The final review is at the corporate level. The summation of corporate plans, largely in financial form, is a five-year forecast of the several national economies in which the corporation has a significant stake, an overview of conformity with environmental regulations, a discussion of probable new regulatory actions, a presentation by the corporate engineering department, a human resource report, and analysis and forecast material of a nature the CEO is more or less used to hearing.

Because the chief technology officer is relatively new to his position and because his plans are in part derivations of the business plans, he defers presenting his plans until the others have been reviewed, modified if necessary, and adopted.

Over the next two weeks the CEO meets frequently with his executive committee (the chief operating officer, CTO, chief financial officer, director of human resources, and strategic planner) to deliberate the many challenges, amplifications, and clarifications and to discuss management talent. In the end he has one overriding worry, which he expresses in this way: "As you know, this is my first venture into the leadership of a company that relies heavily on R&D for its future prosperity. Indeed, Intercontinental relies about $170 million on R&D, not including the work done in Central Research. That amount will, by plan, grow at roughly the rate of inflation. The sum represents a major proportion of forecast annual earnings and much more than we will pay out to shareholders. In the case of two or three businesses, the forecast R&D expenditures drive them into the red for the next two or three years.

"In the ten days of reviews, and in the follow-on discussions, I reckon that we have spent 50 or 60 hours talking about markets, marketing, and sales; we have spent 10 or 15 hours on manufacturing and production investment requirements. But how much time did we devote to R&D? Probably an hour, maybe two.

"Most of the division presidents treat R&D as a line item, more or less the way they treat taxes and with just about as much respect. In six of the nine meetings, the divisional director of R&D was not invited. The divisions that did get into some depth were those with the larger charges for R&D and those whose earnings were the most seriously compromised by those charges. But how illuminating were those discussions?

"They contained language I could not understand. The division presidents declared that R&D was critical to their businesses but did not explain why. They talked of novelty and opportunity and the impossibility of timing creativity and inventions. They implied that faith is the key dimension in R&D funding and that, if we all have faith, all will be wonderful—but at some indeterminate future time.

"I don't buy it.

"Do not conclude from my comments that my executive capabilities are limited by my lack of technical background. Let me remind you that James Webb, Kennedy's head of NASA in the 1960s, was a lawyer. He ran one of the most complicated technological enterprises of all time, and he put men on the moon on time and on budget. Irving Shapiro of Du Pont was a lawyer.

"I think these people control R&D on more than just faith."

He turns to the chief technologist.

"As of this moment, you are CTO not just for Central Research—whatever that is—but for the entire corporation. I want you to make sense of this for me, this committee, and the divisions. In the meantime, we'll proceed with divisional R&D plans as presented, because I see no other choice for the present.

"When can I have your results?"

There is a significant pause before the CTO replies: "First, I think your attitude is constructive and perceptive. Many CEOs also treat R&D as a tax, an unavoidable evil. In fact, in our kinds of businesses, it can be and should be a competitive weapon. Second, I can't give you what I think you mean by 'results' that convey to you in a neat package all you ever needed to know about R&D and our businesses. I can, however, begin a process that will put you, this committee, and the division presidents in a position to make informed, intelligent, strategic judgments about R&D."

"I guess I was hoping for a two-page summary of R&D value for each business," the CEO replies. "But let's do it your way."

"The first step is to get on your calendar," the CTO says. "This responsibility is too important for you to leave it to me. I will do all the detail and background work, but the demand for business impact from R&D, for profitability from an annual $200 million in R&D investment, must come from you."

"Conceptually, that's true. But my time is limited, and I don't know anything about R&D except that it's very expensive."

"First, you don't need to understand the technologies in any detail. That is desirable, of course, but not essential. You do need to grasp their potential impact on our businesses. And I promise you the return on your time investment will be huge."

"Is this one of those tricks of delegating responsibility upward?" the CEO asks.

"Not in the slightest. Only you can articulate and control a strategic vision for Intercontinental. Only you can mobilize all the resources needed to make that vision a reality. Only you have the clout to make fundamental change happen. You are like the leader of a country engaged in a war. You must set the strategic objectives of the war. Then the rest of us go to battle and make it happen."

"Okay, but if you come into my office spouting technical jargon and try to snow me, I'll throw you back to a research bench."

The first meeting between the CTO and the still skeptical CEO occurs three days later. It is scheduled for the last two hours of a Friday. The CTO brings four charts (appearing later as Figures 4-2,

4-3, 4-4, and 4-5) and, to the CEO's relief, no reports, no computer printouts, no planning documents, and no books of R&D projects.

"I thought we would start with a real-world example, using one of the division's business plans, to illustrate some key principles of R&D planning," the CTO begins. "I chose the Haber Food Ingredients Division because its R&D and technology needs are pretty broad. They illustrate the key strategic points you should consider and the strategic directions you must set. Please remember, however, that although the R&D planning principles—the strategic principles—are constant from division to division, the different industries they represent require different levels and types of R&D.

"Haber packages and sells its own products—or sometimes buys and repackages products manufactured by other companies—to companies in the processed food and beverage industry like Kraft and Campbell Soup. These are often key ingredients to consumer products. Haber offers scores of products, many of them tailored to precise customer requirements. All have certain R&D needs in common; but they are clustered roughly into five categories of products, each cluster having its own special R&D needs. I've prepared a chart that shows the five [see Figure 4-2].

"Please note that each cluster is characterized by a certain range of gross contribution to profit. In a minute I'll show you why the margins differ and why each category demands a different kind and level of R&D support."

"Well," says the CEO, smiling, "just tell R&D to deliver more products in the 50 percent margin range and I'll be generous with them."

"I wish it were that simple," the CTO replies, "but look at the absolute contributions to gross profit."

"You don't have to say anything," the CEO says. "I see the point. Vanillin, with a gross margin of 16 percent, makes a lot more money than the cheese flavor, with a margin nearly twice as high."

"Right. And if I added a column for return on equity (ROE), the matter would become even more complex. In short, you cannot tell a priori from numbers like these what, if anything, you should spend on R&D and toward what goals.

"Look at my next chart [see Figure 4-3]. It gives a brief overview of some critical business strategies for each product cluster—addressing the key bases of competition—which suggest the correct R&D work they should drive.

"The food-ingredients industry demands a high level of customer

Figure 4-2

Haber Food Ingredients Division

Sales, Margins, and Profits by Product

Product Cluster	Products	Annual Sales ($MM)	Gross Margin %	Gross Profit ($MM)	Technological Bases of Competition
1	Vanillin (synthetic)	120	16	19	Cost; technical service to customers
	Citric acid (purchased for resale)	50	14	7	
2	Cola concentrates	64	22	14	Formulation and sensory skills; technical service to customers; price; cost; steady stream of new products
	Fruit syrup concentrates	53	23	12	
3	Essence of natural butter flavor	80	31	25	Performance superiority; formulation and sensory skills; all natural; technical service to customers; price; cost; new products
	Essence of natural cheese flavor	40	30	12	
4	Sweetane	110	53	58	Performance superiority; technical service to customers; price; cost; new products
	Enzyme Alpha	83	51	42	
5	Enzyme Beta	0	Experimental; goal=50%	—	Goal: low-calorie fat substitute; safety; performance
	Cocoa butter	100	Now 22%; goal= 40-60%	22	Cost; uniformity; technical service to customers
	TOTAL	$700	30%	$211	

service. Service is an indispensable component of success. Customers expect our reps to work side by side with their R&D people, in *their* labs, as well as in our own, to develop the best overall product formulations. Customer service shows up as a key R&D contribution in every one of the five categories of products, albeit at different levels of relative importance in each. Of the $18 million or so in R&D for the division, about $7 million is for customer service. Although it is really neither research nor development in a pure sense, it is a technical expense and is included within the R&D budget for administrative and tax reasons.

"Service represents the common R&D contribution to success within all of the five clusters. Now let's look at those elements of R&D that the different competitive characteristics of each category demand.

"Cluster one is represented by vanillin and citric acid. These are

48

Figure 4-3

Haber Food Ingredients Division

General Business Strategies by Product Cluster

Product Cluster	Products	Business Strategy
1	**Commodity ingredients** Vanillin (synthetic) Citric acid (purchased for resale)	• Vanillin: achieve cost leadership; increase market share • Citric acid: maintain as service to customers
2	**Flavor extracts** Cola concentrates Fruit syrup concentrates	• Expand by additions to current product line
3	**Natural flavor essences** Essence of natural butter flavor Essence of natural cheese flavor	• Maintain excellence of essences of butter and cheese • Expand by development of new, proprietary natural flavor essences
4	**Proprietary specialty products** Sweetane Enzyme Alpha	• Expand both by intensified marketing, sales, and service; renew proprietary product line
5	**New business ventures** Enzyme Beta Cocoa butter	• Accelerate Enzyme Beta for production of noncaloric fat substitute • Diversify product portfolio within food-ingredients industry with proprietary, high-value-in-use products
	All businesses	• Maintain superior capability and capacity in technical service to customers

commodity products, identical to competitors' offerings. Indeed, as long as they satisfy FDA regulations, they will not be different from those of our competitors. Inevitably, the bases of competition are price and service. We make our own vanillin because we have a good manufacturing process, maybe even better than our competitors', so our costs are good. We buy and resell citric acid because we can't compete either in the technology of its manufacture or on the immense scale of Pfizer, our supplier. Incidentally, despite the business differences, the return on equity for the two is the same—about 20 percent.

"The applications of vanillin and citric acid are decades old, well understood in the industry, and widespread. So it is unlikely that we can develop important new markets for them. The R&D emphasis, if any at all, can be only on cost of manufacture for such commodities."

The CTO goes on to explain that the two examples in the second cluster—flavor compounds—require different kinds of R&D support. Although their price to the customer is important, it isn't decisive. Flavor compounds demand rather sophisticated formulation skills, sometimes involving combinations of 12 or 15 ingredients, to arrive at the balance of freshness, sweetness, tartness, aroma, mouthfeel, and the like sought by the customer. The formulation skills demand support from a sophisticated, highly experienced function in R&D called the Sensory Group.

"Sensory?" the CEO says quizzically.

"Sensory refers to highly developed, highly trained tasting and olfactory skills. These people have palates and noses so refined, so well trained, that they can detect and often identify components you *don't* want in a flavor at a level of a few parts per million, as well as those you need to achieve the desired richness, fullness, and balance.

"These competitive characteristics—performance based on formulation and sensory skills, at which we are sharper than nearly all of our competitors—in addition to price and service, explain our higher margins and give us the first indication of the correct investment of R&D funds."

"Are these sensory people better than all of those expensive analytical instruments I saw in the labs?"

"For these purposes, infinitely. They really are indispensable resources."

"Okay, go on."

The chief technologist then explains that the third cluster, essences of natural butter and cheese flavors, presents an even more complex challenge to R&D. First, it takes some 20–30 components in each, exquisitely balanced in the formulas, to impart a true butter flavor to margarine or a true cheese flavor to snack food. Second, all the components must be natural. Finding and isolating the components from natural sources test the limits of separation and analytical equipment, and human skills, and all has to be done at acceptable costs. Again, the sensory resource is indispensable.

"Haber is probably the best in the business with these kinds of products," the CTO explains. "And that accounts for the superior margins. Another factor is that we have solid patents on the process we use to isolate a few of the key flavor components."

"I think you are telling me that the implications for R&D are to keep up the good job of differentiating us from competitors and that it's worth the investment to do so," the CEO replies.

"Yes and no," the CTO says. "Unfortunately, our competitors

understand the technologies we practice. We think the formulation technologies for these natural flavor essences are mature—that is, nearly exhausted—and not much further advance in the completeness and quality of the essences is likely. Only the patents prevent competitors from closely imitating—even duplicating—our products, and those patents expire in a few years. Then the game may deteriorate to one of cost and price."

"Not my favorite way to compete," the CEO muses.

"The real R&D issue in this cluster of products is whether we should keep intact and strong those excellent R&D resources in natural flavor essences that brought us to where we are and dedicate them to developing proprietary natural essences of other things such as strawberries, peanuts, salmon, or truffles. However, those are not primary R&D questions, but rather market and business questions. Only when those questions have been answered can we talk about what R&D can and should do."

The next subject is the fourth cluster of products, which produces gross margins in the 50 percent range.

"The reason these winners exist will interest you, I'm certain, but the history behind their discovery and development may make you uneasy," the CTO says.

The CTO then explains that Sweetane is a no-calorie sugar substitute, especially effective in cooked products where aspartame, one of its functional competitors, cannot be used. Enzyme Alpha is a natural enzyme that greatly accelerates the aging of cheese so, for example, cheddar aged three months with Enzyme Alpha tastes like cheddar aged a full year without the enzyme.

"About ten years ago, as I understand it, the Haber division began a bold program of exploratory research," the CTO continues. "This was really breakthrough research, whose objectives were proprietary, really profitable new products for Haber. Haber was then a company with modest sales—about $80 million—and even more modest earnings, but great strategic promise.

"Two of the results of that research were Sweetane—a product of good luck, good insight, and great development—and Enzyme Alpha, a product not of luck but of exceptional skill and commitment and risk taking and development. Sweetane is protected by a very strong composition-of-matter patent that has about ten years to run. Enzyme Alpha is protected by an overlapping set of process-manufacturing patents. So far we have no competitors for either. Both products provide high value-in-use for our customers and, obviously, great value to us.

"That's the good news. The spooky part of the story is that, of eleven exploratory research projects started in that time, ten failed. Only the Enzyme Alpha project succeeded in the original terms of success. Sweetane was discovered in one of the ten failed projects by good luck, or, I might better say, the intelligent use of luck.

"One or two successes out of eleven starts, Mr. CEO. How do you like those odds? Before you answer, let me point out that the earnings from the successes have already paid many times over for the R&D costs of the failures, and they will continue to profit us handsomely for some years."

The discussion that follows is spirited. They talk about risk factors. CEO: "Why didn't we have three or four successes?" CTO: "Better to ask, why did we have even two?"

They philosophize. CEO: "You are arguing that we—or at least Haber—must do its own R&D, that we can't buy results at lower cost and lower risk?" CTO: "Yes, and sometimes we should. But it is difficult to buy technology that will belong exclusively to us and thereby provide proprietary advantage."

They speculate. CEO: "Why can't I move R&D resources from one less promising or less threatened business to another more promising or more threatened business?" CTO: "You can. As we will get into later, that is one of the keys to strategically planned R&D."

The CTO continues, "All these questions are valid. All deserve more thoughtful answers than I've given you. But I suggest that we may be getting ahead of ourselves.

"The last cluster is the really speculative one. The Enzyme Beta project is based on published reports that a certain rare species of South American insect—from the order lepidoptera, which includes butterflies and moths—contains in its gut an enzyme—that is, a complex protein substance that catalyzes life processes. This enzyme converts a common fat into a nondigestible fatlike substance. In other words, Enzyme Beta converts certain high-calorie vegetable oils into a fatlike product that, to humans, looks, tastes, and feels like oil but is not digested in the human system and therefore is calorie free. It is in the earliest stages of research, and the probabilities of the many research successes we need for commercial success are unknown."

"Do you mean," interjects the CEO, "that French fries and butter and ice cream—all those goodies—could be made no-calorie or low calorie? That's really something."

"That's the good part. But please remember, remind yourself every day, that this project is a tremendous long shot. There are many known uncertainties and probably some we don't know yet. The overall probability of technical and commercial success at this time is 10 percent or less.

"If we are extremely smart, and if nature cooperates, and if competitors don't get there first, and if the FDA approves, and if we get the right patents, we are talking five to ten years and tens of millions of dollars before we could bring in the first dollar of revenue."

"Both the risk and the obvious potential reward boggle the mind," the CEO says. "Tell me more. Where does the project stand? Can I see a plan, an analysis? What do we need to do to improve the chances of success and shorten the time?"

"We'll get to all of those issues in good time. I'd like to describe briefly the cocoa butter project before the day ends, and then I'd like to use all of the examples we've discussed to take you to what I believe to be an important set of operating principles—strategic planning principles—that a chief executive should accommodate in his business and corporate strategic thinking.

"The company owns a cocoa plantation in Ghana. The most valuable product of the cocoa bean is cocoa butter, used in the highest quality chocolate confections, some cosmetics, and a few other miscellaneous applications. Its price is determined strictly by supply and demand. Its cost is determined by crop yield, which in turn is governed by environmental factors, chief of which is rainfall.

"In a typical year, a ton of cocoa beans will yield about 1,000 pounds of cocoa butter. We have a research project in place to modify the cocoa tree genetically, with two priority goals: first, to increase the yield of cocoa butter from a ton of beans to 1,300–1,400 pounds; and second, to make the yield less susceptible to variations in rain—in effect, to make the plant more drought resistant. We will have a winner if we achieve either. If we achieve both, we could have a blockbuster."

The CEO shakes his head, whether in dismay or disbelief or shock or fatigue is not clear to the CTO, who quickly adds, "But this is a serious gamble. The genetics of the cocoa tree are only slightly understood. We have indications that these goals are, in principle, achievable. But there is a vast reach from principle to a producing plantation. The stakes are high, the probability of success really unknowable, although surely greater than zero or we wouldn't be in the project.

"On the other hand," the CTO continues, "we are in an early exploratory stage of research now, and the costs are relatively modest, about $1 million a year."

"I don't think I've ever met a modest million dollars," the CEO remarks. "And when do I get to explore this project, or dream, or hallucination, or whatever it is?"

"Soon. The last two efforts—Enzyme Beta and cocoa butter—are mine, that is, in Central Research. We can review them in whatever depth you want when you like. The others are within the Haber Food Ingredients Division, and I can get more detailed information from them, or you can ask them yourself."

"It's 7 o'clock," the CTO says. "Do you want to delay the discussion of the planning principles for which all of this has been introduction until another time?"

"How much longer will the strategic discussion take?"

"Twenty, maybe thirty minutes."

"Okay, let's go."

"Briefly, the R&D options you have for each business are few and they are simple. They apply to every one of Intercontinental's businesses and, indeed, to every business in the world that has an R&D component.

"Basically, there are only three categories of R&D: incremental R&D, radical R&D, and fundamental R&D.

"There is also the area of customer service. It is technical and it is important. It is part of the value we add to Haber's products, and it keeps us in intimate contact with customers, their needs, their plans, and their manufacturing methods; and, not least, it provides important intelligence on competitors' activities. However, it is not 'research' and it is not 'development.' It will not advance the company technologically very much, but it does contribute invaluable intelligence toward making R&D more useful.

"So, there are really only three categories of R&D, and the boundaries between them are indistinct. The three categories represent regions of a spectrum, each connected, perhaps loosely, to the other."

The CTO then explains that the three R&D types, described in Figure 4-4, enclose all of the research conducted in Haber and elsewhere.

"What is the value of this classification? Despite the simplicity of the names, the differences are profound. Each category offers its own standards of reward, cost, risk, and time to usable results, significance of the technological differentiation the results will provide, and possibility of protection. Strategically each has different goals and impact, but strategically each is important.

"And as important as the classification of R&D projects is for

Figure 4-4

Characteristics of three types of R&D

Type of R&D	Characteristics of the Type
Incremental	Normally, the clever exploitation of existing scientific and engineering knowledge in new ways; characterized by low risk and modest reward
Radical	The creation of knowledge new to the company–and possibly new to the world–for a specified business objective; characterized by higher risk and high reward
Fundamental	The creation of knowledge new to the company–and probably new to the world–to broaden and deepen the company's understanding of a scientific or engineering arena; characterized by high risk and uncertain applicability to business needs

consideration of their business and strategic impact, equally important is the need to have an appropriate—let's say an optimum—balance of commitment to them. By that I mean a strategically balanced R&D portfolio and optimum distribution of resources across the three categories depending on the strategic condition of the business, its competitors, its goals, its resources, and the scope of additional, profitable technological advance. But we'll defer the discussion of portfolio balance for now."

"I'm hearing words I understand but I'm not feeling enlightened," the CEO says. "Defer what you need to defer and get on with the significance of the three R&D categories."

"Right. Bear with me a few more moments. I think much more of this will become clear.

"An example of incremental R&D is Haber's work on vanillin. The major basis of competition, in addition to service, is cost and price. Haber has a very good manufacturing process, but it can be improved by a collection of small but meaningful advances. They are probably all cost justified and, in the aggregate, will save about

3 cents per pound of product. And that multiplies to about $4 million a year that Haber can use for an improved margin or for increased market share by more aggressive pricing. Small, incremental technical steps, but with large strategic results.

"The R&D work now being done for cola and fruit syrup concentrates falls roughly in the same category. It is an extension into products with know-how we already possess.

"But there is an important potential difference between future R&D work for vanillin and flavor concentrates, and future work for flavor essences. Vanillin is vanillin; its manufacturing process is old and well established; and the only work we can visualize of any importance for that business is for incremental cost reduction. Flavor concentrates require formulation and sensory skills, but only incrementally.

"The modest amount of R&D now expended for the butter and cheese essences also falls into the category of incremental R&D. On the other hand, if the flavor-essences business decides to add a line of altogether new products—for example, flavor essences of peanuts or shrimp—incremental R&D won't produce them. They would have to come from radical R&D.

"In the case of these new natural flavor essences, research would have to isolate and chemically identify the key flavor and aroma components—maybe between ten and thirty for each essence—learn how to unite them in an essence that would confidently impart the flavor to food products, and discover how to extract each component at a reasonable cost from natural sources, or to manufacture them, possibly by fermentation.

"Finally," the CTO continues, "our current work on Enzyme Beta and the genetics of the cocoa plant is an example of fundamental research, characterized by major uncertainties, long time frames, but the potential for staggering rewards.

"The decision whether or not to invest in fundamental research, and if so, how much and in what fields, is one of the toughest in R&D and corporate planning.

"The answers all hinge on judgment, the corporate culture, and the present and future nature of the technologies that the company will either exploit or be exploited by.

"In fact, most companies—especially smaller ones with sales of less than, say, $1 billion—should probably not invest significant sums in fundamental research. They should closely track research results produced by others such as university researchers. It is possible to be quite innovative without large investments in fundamental research.

"Even Apple Computer, as far as I know, does little fundamental research. But IBM does a lot, as do AT&T and NEC and Sony and Siemens. Will Apple be around in twenty-five years? I don't know, but I think IBM, AT&T, NEC, Sony, and Siemens all will be. What is the inference from this? Perhaps it is my bias, but any company that places its bets on innovation from the fundamental research of others is always at risk. Another company has access to the same knowledge. If they apply the knowledge more quickly, more cunningly . . .

"In chemicals, Germany's Bayer and Hoechst, France's Rhône-Poulenc, Holland's DSM, Britain's ICI, Italy's Montedison-Himont, and the United States's Du Pont and Monsanto all do a lot of fundamental R&D.

"Who will be strong in the year 2010, and who will have disappeared? We can continue with examples you would recognize in industries like machine tools, robotics, automobiles, communications, even home appliances; and in technologies such as ceramics, high-performance plastics, superconductivity, biotechnology, solar energy, coal conversion, natural gas conversions, and many others.

"Who would invest in fundamental research? Should we? If the answer is 'yes,' in what and to what purpose and to what extent? If not, why not?"

"Perhaps I should have stayed in financial services," the CEO says glumly. "Perhaps my ego is bigger than my capacity to learn. Do you really think I can cope with all of this in five divisions, as well as Central Research?"

"Of course you can," the CTO says. "Let me show you a recapitulation of the characteristics of the three categories of R&D expressed in business terms [see Figure 4-5].

"The decision whether or not to undertake radical or fundamental research for a business is one of prime strategic importance. You must answer questions such as these:

- Do we want or need the new products or processes?
- Is there an attractive market for them?
- What are the risks in research, money, and time?
- Can we afford to fund the projects through their full life cycle?
- And if we decide not to go ahead and a competitor does and succeeds, where will that leave us?

Figure 4-5

Characteristics of three types of R&D

Type of R&D	Probability of Technical Success	Time to Completion	Competitive Potential	Durability of Competitive Advantage Gained
Incremental	Very high, typically 40 to 80%	Short, typically 6 to 24 months	Modest, but necessary	Short, typically imitable by competitors
Radical	In early stages modest, typically 20 to 40%	Mid-term, typically 2 to 7 years	Large	Long, often protectable by patents
Fundamental	In early stages difficult to assess; depends on R&D concept	Long, typically 4 to 10 or more years	Large	Long, often protectable by patents

"In Von Clausewitz' construct, the choice of the engagements you can win determines the outcome of the war."

"I'm tired," the CEO says, glancing at his watch. "Good heavens, it's 8:30. I hope your future time forecasts are a little sharper than tonight's." He begins putting papers in his briefcase.

The CTO reaches into his briefcase and offers the CEO a manila file. "Here is a brief overview of the strategic principles we discussed and a new briefing paper. Don't worry, it is short. Like all good operating principles, the content is easy to digest, although the application isn't always simple."

"What a way to start a long holiday weekend," the CEO says, thumbing quickly through the briefing paper. "Good night. Next week, we need to start thinking about strategy."

Note

1. Claude von Clausewitz, *On War* (Princeton, NJ: Princeton University Press, 1989).

Briefing Paper 1

Technology, Maturation, and Competitive Impact

The concept of technological maturity places a technology along a continuum of technological advance and helps one understand the possibilities for additional advances in the technology. Like living organisms, technologies have life cycles, from birth to old age.

At birth, a new technology is called embryonic. At this stage, a vision of possible practical application exists, but so little of a practical nature is known that the route of future development from vision to industrial reality is, at best, cloudy. The embryonic stage is one of substantial scientific tumult and contradiction, but if it seems promising enough to enough bright minds, an embryonic technology attracts the attention and the research energy of laboratories all over the world.

The accuracy of the vision for practical applications of a technology in the embryonic state is typically suspect, hardly surprising in view of the modest level of scientific understanding that, by definition, characterizes this stage.

For example, in the case of the embryonic stage of recombinant DNA technology—one component of the revolution commonly called biotechnology—visions ranged from (1) the search simply to understand the possibility of modifying bacteria to produce useful therapeutic substances such as insulin and human growth hormone (for the treatment of dwarfism), instead of relying on animal sources; to (2) the search for a process to convert cellulose not digestible by humans (such as hay) to edible products digestible by humans, with great benefit to humankind; to (3) the low-cost transformation of natural gas and coproducts to animal feed; to (4) highly specific anticancer substances that would attack and detoxify cancer cells while leaving normal cells untouched.

In the case of embryonic biotechnology, the visions of practical applications were immediately compelling. Within a few years of the discovery in 1974 of practical means to experiment in the field, scores of university and government laboratories, and uncounted companies, were investing enormous sums in R&D to advance and apply the new technology. That research ferment attracted many of the best scientists and a good deal of venture capital, which in a few years expanded the knowledge base to the point where biotechnology moved into the next phase of technological maturity, the growth stage.

In the growth stage of technological maturity, so much knowledge is accumulated and disseminated that the projection of what can be accomplished in a practical technological sense is sharpened from the murky vision that characterized the embryonic stage to much more realistic forecasts. In this growth stage, much technological uncertainty remains and much R&D advance still lies ahead, but much uncertainty has been erased.

Applications that are practical come into sharper view, and enough knowledge exists to begin abandoning the impractical. In the case of biotechnology, the manufacture of insulin and human growth hormone became realities; the products are in the therapeutic repertory. Work on the transformation of cellulose to food digestible by humans, an improbable dream, has virtually ceased. The conversion of natural gas and coproducts to animal feed succeeded technically but was a financial failure.

With continued investment in R&D, the technology advances into the mature stage, where the pace of advance in understanding and development slows, the magnitude of each new advance is not as profound, and the basic technologies become well understood by R&D organizations around the world. The fundamentals of the mature technology will be taught in high school science classes. There will still be technological advances in the mature stage, but they will tend to be less revolutionary and more predictable.

In biotechnology, the technology associated with cloning by hybridoma methods to reproduce identical cells that produce identical products has entered the early part of the mature stage. By now, it is widely understood and practiced in many sophisticated laboratories.

Inevitably, with time and continued investment in R&D, technologies advance to the aging stage, characterized by substantial completion of scientific and engineering advance. Advance is still possible, but each advance will represent a small increment, one that is highly predictable and, in industry, easily and quickly imitated by competitors.

No element of biotechnology is close to the aging stage yet. But many other technologies illustrate the point. The thermal pasteurization of milk is at the extreme of the aging stage, and no responsible

Figure Briefing 1-1

Technologies can be characterized by their maturities

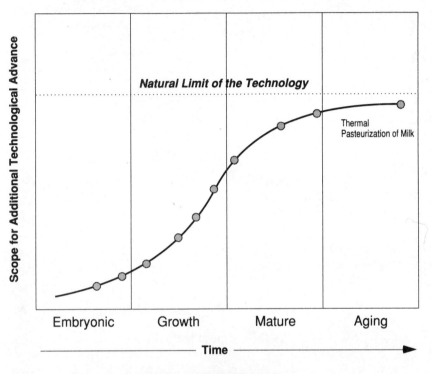

Technological Maturity

Source: Adapted from Philip A. Roussel, "Technological Maturity Proves a Valid and Important Concept," *Research Management*, vol. 27, no. 1 (January –February 1984), p. 30.

R&D organization will invest in advancing it because there are no meaningful advances left to be made. However, this is not true for the makers of pasteurization equipment. They will continue to make advances in equipment for better control, faster throughput, easier cleanup, and better suppression of biological contamination.

The process of technology maturation is often represented by a curve such as that shown in Figure Briefing 1-1, which expresses the state of technology knowledge and the possibilities for additional advances through the four stages of maturity as a function of time. The curve is an idealized one. In the real world of technology, the climb toward maturity is a series of steps contributed to by hundreds

Figure Briefing 1-2

Technologies can be characterized by their maturities

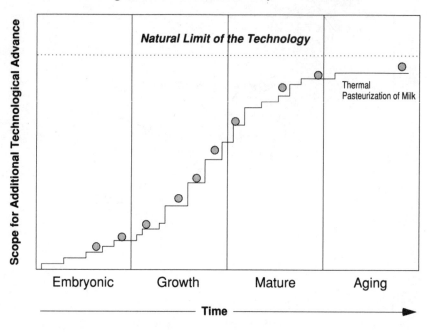

Technological Maturity

or thousands of researchers. Thus, the technological maturity curve is better represented in Figure Briefing 1-2.

The generalized characteristics of technology maturity are summarized in Figure Briefing 1-3. For strategic planning in R&D, the maturity of the technologies in which a company invests drives highly important consequences and must be incorporated in prudent R&D plans. Technological maturity helps define

- Uncertainty/risk
- Reward
- Competitive activity
- Probability of success
- Management expectations
- Accountability
- Appropriate R&D strategies
- Marketing and investment strategies

Figure Briefing 1-3

Characteristics of R&D as a function of technological maturity

Technological Maturity	Time to Commercial- ization	Knowledge of Competitive R&D	Predictability			Durability of Commercial Advantage
			Technical	Reward	R&D Costs	
Embryonic	7-15 years	Poor	Poor	Fair	Poor	High
Growth	2-7 years	Fair-Moderate	Fair	High	Moderate	Moderate
Mature	1-4 years	High	High	High	High	Fair
Aging	1-4 years	High	Very High	Very High	Very High	Short

Source: Adapted from Philip A. Roussel, "Technological Maturity Proves a Valid and Important Concept," *Research Management,* vol. 27, no. 1 (January –February 1984), p. 30.

Progress up the technological maturity curve toward the natural limit of the technology applies to a well-defined technology or set of technologies—for example, the technologies embodied in a mechanical watch. As technologies age, it is common for new technologies to enter the field, as the electronic watch did in the portable timepiece industry. When the electronic watch entered the competitive arena, it was based on a growth technology that competitors all over the globe advanced and exploited to seize the advantage over mechanical watches. The technologies of mechanical watches were aging, and the manufacturers could not update them with technological advances.

Similarly, as the technology for the manufacture of latex foam cushioning matured, the new technology of polyurethane foam appeared to challenge it. Today, there is a mammoth polyurethane cushioning foam industry, and virtually no latex foam manufacture remains.

The new technology represented by the antiulcer drug Tagamet has virtually eliminated the old technology—surgery—for duodenal ulcers.

The aging technologies of glass container manufacturing have been mauled by a class of packaging plastics.

Figure Briefing 1-4

Competitive impact of technologies

Descriptor	Competitive Impact
Pacing Technology	• Technologies that have the potential to change the entire basis of competition but have not yet been embodied in a product or process • These technologies often develop into key technologies
Key Technology	• Technologies that are most critical to competitive success because they offer the opportunity for meaningful process or product differentiation • These technologies yield competitive advantage
Base Technology	• Technologies that, although necessary and essential to practice well, offer little potential for competitive advantage • These technologies are typically widespread and shared

The tiring technologies of aluminum in aircraft manufacture are being attacked by lightweight composite organic structures.

The litany of such displacements of mature-to-aging technologies by upstart new ones is nearly endless and is to be watched carefully in the construction of a superior R&D portfolio. Richard Foster's *Innovation: The Attacker's Advantage*[1] offers many examples of technologies approaching their limits supplanted by younger and more vigorous ones, often from outside the industry.

Like technological maturity, a second R&D planning concept, the competitive impact of technologies, seen in Figure Briefing 1-4, provides valuable insights into the nature of R&D that should be undertaken and R&D that should not. There is a natural progression in the competitive impact of technologies, typically represented by a progression over time from pacing to key to base technologies (see Figure Briefing 1-5). Technological maturity is intrinsic to a technology, regardless of the industry in which it is applied. The competitive impact of a technology is extrinsic, the impact closely dependent on the industry that applies it.

The first mechanical typewriters reflected young and key technologies—the translation of the mechanical action of fingers into printed type—vastly superior to the pen they displaced. Over time, those mechanical technologies aged and decayed to base technologies well known and practiced by all competitors. In time, the electric typewriter incorporated some new and key technologies to displace

Figure Briefing 1-5

The typical progression of the competitive impact of technologies over time

COMPETITIVE IMPACT OF TECHNOLOGIES

Pacing →	Key →	Base
Potential to change the basis of technological competition	Embodied in products and processes, differentiated in leading companies	Essential, but known to and practiced by all competitors

————————————————— Time —————————————————→

the mechanical systems. Then those technologies were displaced by R&D effort into the key technologies that made possible the electric typewriter's successors, the word processor and even personal computers now at every secretary's desk, far superior to all of their predecessor instruments and not really "typewriters" at all.

One can trace this inexorable march of technology in every industry. Compare the 35mm camera of today with the best of twenty years ago. And television, automobiles, antibiotics, blood analyzers, food processing, tires, microcircuits, computers, oil exploration, pollution control—the list is nearly endless.

Simply stated, the strategic mission of R&D is to exploit the potential for improvement in competitive position in technologies that are important to the business. These are first and foremost key technologies, then pacing technologies, and, always, competence in base technologies.

The maturities of technologies in the business provide insights into the potential for future technological advances. The competitive impacts of those technologies indicate the differences that such advances might make to specific businesses in specific industries. The two concepts—technological maturity and technological competitive impact—and how well they are mastered are clearly basic to effective R&D planning.

Note

1. Richard Foster, *Innovation: The Attacker's Advantage* (New York: Summit Books, 1986).

Chapter 5

Evaluating Risks and Rewards

R&D produces one product only—knowledge. True, it is knowledge with a purpose, but it is still just knowledge. R&D does not produce sales, earnings, or cost reduction. It does not produce a physical product for sale or an operating process. It does not produce a new business. Nor does it produce quality. However, R&D does produce the know-how at the foundation of all of these other results.

In almost all companies, across the world, the know-how developed by R&D must be translated by management action into products, processes, cost reductions, quality improvements, conformance with environmental regulations, support of product claims, and other objectives. Rarely is this know-how created strictly for sale.

In short, R&D seeks out the location of the treasure, but senior business management holds the keys to it. Only management can mobilize all of the resources necessary to transform an R&D result—knowledge—into a commercially useful result. Only management can provide the support from marketing, manufacturing, or capital. Only management can enforce the company's vision and strategies and involve all functions—including R&D—in their successful implementation.

Intercontinental's new CEO has begun to understand this fundamental principle. He has a grasp of the three classifications of R&D—incremental, radical, and fundamental—and their differentiating characteristics. He understands how customer service relates to R&D.

But what does he actually know when he accepts those classifications? The characteristics of R&D described by the chief technology officer tell him a great deal. But what they do not tell him troubles him.

The three types of R&D don't tell him the R&D strategies each division should pursue. Therefore, they don't tell him how to judge the R&D plans in place at each division and in Central Research, how well integrated the business and R&D plans are, or how for-

Figure 5-1

Haber Food Ingredients Division

General Business Strategies by Product Cluster

Product Cluster	Products	Business Strategy
1	**Commodity ingredients** Vanillin (synthetic) Citric acid (purchased for resale)	• Vanillin: achieve cost leadership; increase market share • Citric acid: maintain as service to customers

ward looking. The categories and characteristics certainly don't reveal how much to spend on R&D in each business.

But the CEO feels he can delay that decision. He will let that decision rise out of the strategic considerations. He wonders if, in those long hours of briefings, his CTO simply gave him business school theory and if theory, as appealing as it may be, can be transformed into plans and action.

In some ways, the CEO's distress is well founded. He has in his possession some useful concepts and principles, in effect a new planning and communications tool. But the instructions for using the tool are lacking. It is as if he has a set of high-quality wrenches without any clue as to which bolts need to be tightened, which loosened, and which left alone.

But in other ways the CEO's distress is unjustified. In fact, the principles given him by his CTO embody implicit instructions on the uses of the planning tools. As he muses further about the utility of the concepts and their practical application within Intercontinental, he shifts his thinking from the general to the particular. He consults the few charts his chief technologist left with him during the first day of briefings.

In cluster 1 (see Figure 5-1), represented by vanillin and citric acid, the key bases of competition on a technological basis are customer service, price, and, indirectly, cost. Haber's R&D addresses all of them. Haber has in place incremental R&D efforts (small "r," large "D"), development efforts that are straightforward, low risk, and offering good potential return to lower the cost of manufacture of vanillin by several million dollars a year. The business can apply those cost savings to earnings or to gain market share—good strategic options. In short, there seems to be a close connection between the needs of the business and the R&D effort—close integration between the bases of competition, the business strategy such as he understands it, and the R&D projects. The incremental nature of the R&D commitment seems, on the surface at least, appropriate.

For a moment the CEO is satisfied with the integration he perceives between business strategy and R&D strategy. His satisfaction, however, is brief. "What if the competitor is developing an altogether new manufacturing process for vanillin, one whose costs are so low that the competitor will make our process obsolete?" he asks himself. He ponders particularly the possibility that a Japanese company, eyeing a large, established stable market, might again be attracted to develop more highly efficient manufacture, a leapfrog process that, given the key cost/price basis of competition, might leave Haber with investment to write off and its $20 million or so in earnings only a memory.

Has Haber been complacent? He resolves to find out and to confirm through his CTO the reality of this threat.

Nevertheless, given all that he heard, the CEO is reasonably satisfied that, once the factors for successful competition have been clearly defined for this business, the linkage between the business strategy and the R&D strategy is not bad and incremental R&D may indeed represent the correct level of R&D commitment, combining low risk with quite satisfactory return, to support that business. He smiles with the satisfaction that he has made the transition rather easily from R&D principle to executive appraisal of a combined business/R&D strategy. Still, there is that nagging sense of risk or uncertainty about the possibility of a competitive attack at the very foundation of vanillin's success.

He moves to the second cluster of Haber's business, flavor extracts (see Figure 5-2). The R&D contributions and the specific R&D objectives for Haber that were described to him seem consistent, integrated, and mutually supporting—one tightly linked business/ R&D strategy. Even so, he is uneasy. All of the R&D work is clearly of an incremental nature. He accepts the premise that Haber's R&D organization offers superior technical service to customers and possesses rare expertise in the sensory business. But aren't these "base" technologies, necessary technical skills but insufficient to protect the business in the face of a determined competitor? Couldn't a determined competitor establish the same skills, then deploy a stronger force of those skills and begin to displace Haber's flavor concentrates or, at minimum, force competition more on the basis of price? Gross

Figure 5-2

Haber Food Ingredients Division

General Business Strategies by Product Cluster

Product Cluster	Products	Business Strategy
2	**Flavor extracts** Cola concentrates Fruit syrup concentrates	• Expand by additions to current product line

margins are only in the 20 percent range. Serious new price competition could drive them to unacceptable levels.

The twin specters of risk and uncertainty again push aside his earlier satisfaction with the integration of business and R&D strategies. In this instance, his concern turns not on the risk associated with the R&D projects in place but with the R&D work that Haber is not doing, the work that would provide more secure, lasting product differentiation and happier margins.

A question gnaws at him. Is Haber being too conservative? Is there a place in the flavor-concentrates business for radical R&D? Vaguely dissatisfied with the risks of prosecuting only incremental R&D, he finds himself attracted, at least in principle, to another kind of risk, that which attends radical R&D. He is conscious, of course, that he must assume objectives with a balance of reward, cost, risk, and time. And Haber must either possess or be able to acquire the right technical skills to carry out such projects.

He wonders if the division is milking the business, adding to its near-term bottom line by avoiding more far-reaching—radical—R&D and its attendant costs and deferred earnings. He adds to his notes the need to discuss this discomfort with Haber and to check the division's responses with his CTO. Perhaps the flavor-concentrates business management was correct. Perhaps there was no place for differentiating radical R&D. But he would like the option to consider such work if "reasonable" opportunities for advance can be identified.

He adds at the bottom of the page on flavor concentrates: "Maybe these simple ideas of incremental, radical, and fundamental R&D are more than pretty theoretical constructs. *Maybe they are actually useful.*"

Figure 5-3

Haber Food Ingredients Division

General Business Strategies by Product Cluster

Product Cluster	Products	Business Strategy
3	**Natural flavor essences** Essence of natural butter flavor Essence of natural cheese flavor	• Maintain excellence of essences of butter and cheese • Expand by development of new, proprietary natural flavor essences

The third cluster of products, under the heading "Natural flavor essences"—mainly the essences of butter and cheese—presents the CEO with an interesting contrast (see Figure 5-3). Within this business the assurances to the CEO are that of product positions protected, at least for the present, by patents, and of products that are of first quality and are purchased by customers for first-line products of their own. Because of this quality and protection, margins are good. But patents expire, and then the vultures descend. Indeed, the vultures begin circling their feast even before the formal demise of patent security, knowing that most companies will not undertake costly litigation to enforce patents during the last two or three years of their viability.

The analysis he had seen projected a good level of patent security for six or seven years. Because of some unprincipled competitors, he reckons a reasonable defense for four years and after that trouble and declining prices.

Both of the flavor-essence products were the result of radical R&D prosecuted by bold or lucky Haber researchers in the past. He regrets that those people are faceless and even nameless to him. Their efforts reflect the kind of vision and thrust and investment in the future that appeals to him. Because of that foresight, the business and the corporation today enjoy the benefits of investments that were no doubt risky and compromising to earnings of the time, especially given a lower sales base then.

He thinks to himself: "Don't I and doesn't Haber's business leadership have the responsibility to expand the company's leadership in flavor essences to the future reward of the division and the corporation—especially in view of the predictable decline in profits from those products as patents approach expiration? After all, I am responsible not simply for protecting the earnings I have but for increasing them."

The CEO rises from his desk and paces for a moment. "You know," he says to no one, "a fool could be CEO and make this company's performance—and himself—look brilliant for a few years. All he needs to do is cut out, say, $25 million a year in R&D costs in the first year and add those dollars to his earnings. What an appearance of growth! Wall Street would love him!"

He knows that few would notice that the price of that short-term "brilliance" would probably be a third-rate company—perhaps even a moribund one—in ten years. The CEO returns to his desk, his briefing materials, and his note pad.

It seems clear that radical R&D and smart business exploitation of its results have gotten the flavor-essence business to its present condition. But where and how to proceed from here? He has the choice of continuing to spend, even to squander, his inheritance, as some legatees and some companies do, or of expanding it.

In principle, he knows the correct course. But how to transform principle into action eludes him for the moment. The business is at risk—future risk, to be sure—but real risk nonetheless. From where is growth to come?

The CEO consults his briefing paper. His memory is correct. The R&D skills that have led to the technical and business successes represented now by butter and cheese essences still exist, more or less, although not as a coherent, focused organizational entity. Would it be wrong to let time and circumstances dissipate those skills? Would it be right to reassemble them, if necessary, and apply them to new opportunities in natural flavor essences? If the latter, what new opportunities?

He recalls his CTO's briefing on the subject. Technically in this field, many R&D projects are doable, albeit with some risk. His notes remind him that the probability of technical success in radical work of this kind might be as low as 20 or 30 percent. Given the demonstration from the past of the value of this work, he can accept that kind of technical risk.

But what of commercial risk? The answer is clear: the business, not R&D, must define the commercial opportunities in natural flavor essences. Then, collectively, business managers and R&D managers can decide whether the technical risk, market opportunity, and commercial risk justify a radical R&D thrust.

He wonders how well equipped Haber is to seek out and evaluate new business opportunities, especially those that would be available five or six years hence, when radical new products from R&D might be ready for production and sale. He has been burned more than a few times by market research studies seeking to project new product needs so far into the future.

On the other hand, he reasons, the pace of change in the processed-food industry is not as rapid as it is in, say, consumer electronics or the medical instrumentation business of the Medelectronics Division. That division's R&D needs will be vastly different from those of Haber. But his reverie does not close the gap in the issue of the future of the flavor essences. So he turns to the subject of technical and commercial risk, and time.

He realizes that, in addition to the R&D and commercial risks that would characterize radical R&D to develop new flavor essences, there are the inevitable uncertainties of the economy five or six years later, of government attitudes, of social conditions and preferences, and of competitors' actions. He is acutely aware that uncertainty about future conditions increases exponentially with time.

He can project with some confidence the major social, political, competitive, and economic conditions that will prevail and affect his company in the next year. He would feel reasonably secure about two years hence. But five or ten years out is a problem. What if he could reduce uncertainty by reducing the time-to-market by accelerating R&D, accelerating market tests, and accelerating market introductions? If, for new flavor essences, time-to-market could be reduced from five or six years to, say, three or four years, his level of business confidence would rise by a factor of two or three.

He jots on his note pad: "Explore what it takes to speed up radical R&D, cut time in half. Good for Haber, especially good for Medelectronics."

He turns to cluster 4, Sweetane and Enzyme Alpha (see Figure 5-4). "What sweet businesses," he thinks.

The CEO recalls that they are the products of a substantial portfolio of radical, and perhaps even fundamental, R&D projects, most of which failed in their intended objectives. The two successes, however, have overwhelmingly paid the cost of the failures and now are rewarding their investors handsomely.

He wonders what R&D is being undertaken to follow up on those compelling successes, to support the present business, and to prepare for the expiration of their precious patents. He supposes that the fundamental research on Enzyme Beta and on cocoa butter produc-

Figure 5-4

Haber Food Ingredients Division

General Business Strategies by Product Cluster

Product Cluster	Products	Business Strategy
4	**Proprietary specialty products** Sweetane Enzyme Alpha	• Expand both by intensified marketing, sales, and service; renew proprietary product line

tion are examples (see Figure 5-5). Is the enzyme science that produced Alpha applicable to the enzyme science that will be necessary to research and develop Beta? He hopes so and vaguely feels that it should be so. "Use strength to build strength," he murmurs. "It must be as true in research as it is in marketing and manufacturing."

The CEO remembers some phrases from his CTO's briefing that somehow take on special meaning. They run something like this: "R&D inevitably entails risk—some element of probability that you will succeed and some that you will fail. That is in the nature of R&D. If you do the obvious and the easy, which involve little risk, you won't fail in your R&D, but you might fail in your business. And remember, what you don't do may entail risks as large as or greater than what you choose to do. These failures will simply be more obscure, less easy to point a finger at. Failures of omission are the way many CEOs, especially American CEOs, protect their backs. Observers often fail to note that, while the CEO's back is secure, his company is slowly growing weaker."

The characteristics of fundamental R&D, the CEO remembers,

Figure 5-5

Haber Food Ingredients Division

General Business Strategies by Product Cluster

Product Cluster	Products	Business Strategy
5	**New business ventures** Enzyme Beta Cocoa butter	• Accelerate Enzyme Beta for production of noncaloric fat substitute • Diversify product portfolio within food-ingredients industry with proprietary, high-value-in-use products

are extremely high risk, long time frames; the probability of very high costs; and highly speculative, highly uncertain commercial outcomes. Before his discussions with the CTO, he could not have guessed that the food-ingredients business could possibly justify that kind of high-risk R&D. But a noncaloric fat! That does engage the imagination. And the cocoa butter thing. Those are the products of which business dreams are made. Think of the distinction to the company if they are successful. Think of Wall Street's reaction if either is. And if both are successes, think of the effect on share prices.

"Yes," he says aloud, "and think of the costs and risks. The costs come directly out of my earnings. They directly, immediately reduce my bottom line. They can reduce investor interest and raise the cost of capital, even if I explain the long-term nature of a potential profit of staggering proportions. With the performance record of this company, will Wall Street be with me or against me? Will investors and analysts embrace me more warmly if I do invest in these fundamental ventures, at a price, or if I don't, with better short-term earnings?"

Since, in his mind, the single consistent characteristic of stock analysts is fickleness, the CEO dimisses further consideration—for the present—of their reactions. The risk/reward decisions belong to him, not to distantly interested analysts who can shift position every quarter without having to account for real results. The proper balance between short-term and long-term results, risk, security, and reward must be found by him and the board of directors. There, in R&D as elsewhere, is where he must focus his energies.

The terms *risk* and *uncertainty* came up repeatedly in the CEO's musings. His chief technologist frequently used *risk* as a strategic descriptor.

Are *risk* and *uncertainty* synonyms? the CEO wonders. And is there anything to be gained in strategy by drawing a distinction between them?

The CEO does a little exercise.

"I cannot know who will be the candidates for president of the country one or two terms from now. I do not know what major conditions will prevail in religion, education, gross domestic product, inflation, music, interest rates, geopolitical relationships, fashion, or diet at that time. Thus I must deal today with a condition of significant uncertainty about that time six or eight years from now when the second of those elections comes up."

Interestingly, six or eight years happens to be about the same reach into time it is reasonable to demand of strategic plans and—is it coincidental?—the same reach into time for the fruition of most radical and fundamental R&D projects. Whether the congruence is accidental or not, the CEO enjoys the discovery.

Uncertainty and risk. Does he have a description of the difference between them? And is that difference a key to effective planning? A scholar of the topic, Donald A. Schon, distinguishes between risk and uncertainty in this way:

> Risk has its place in a calculus of probabilities. It lends itself to quantitative expression—as when we say that the chances of finding a defective part in a batch are two out of 100. In the framework of benefit-cost analysis, the risk of an innovation is how much we stand to lose if we fail, multiplied by the probability of the failure.
>
> Uncertainty is quite another matter. . . . For example, a gambler takes a risk in an honest game of blackjack when, knowing the odds, he calls for another card. But the same gambler, unsure of the odds, or unsure of the honesty of the game, is in a situation of uncertainty.[1]

Schon relates the difference in meaning between *risk* and *uncertainty* to research planning and technical innovation:

> Men involved in technical innovation in a corporation confront a situation in which the need for action is clear but the action itself is not. So long as this situation exists, the corporation cannot function effectively, because it is not designed for uncertainty—a situation in which there are no clear objectives to reach, no measures of accomplishments, and no proper concept of control. A corporation cannot operate in uncertainty, but it is beautifully equipped to handle risk. It is precisely an organization designed to uncover, analyze, evaluate, and operate on risks.[2]

The assertion that a corporation is "beautifully equipped to handle risk" is, of course, open to question, but the CEO knows that it is certainly better equipped if its members recognize the true nature of business risk and apply the term with a meaning common to all.

Risk is a function of the probability of the desired outcome of a defined action (the uncertainty factor) and exposure (typically finan-

cial). "Ah, yes," the CEO says to himself. "The difference between uncertainty and risk is clear. I cannot meaningfully reduce all uncertainties. I can manage risks. I can make my plans according to scenarios rather than explicit forecasts of the future. And the plans can be robust and dynamic enough to move with the inevitable uncertainties of a five-year future."

The CEO accepts what seems to him the essence of the message. Uncertainty is ever present, but, in many instances, it can be restated or reconceptualized as risk. He feels confident that he and his executives can deal with risk. Risk can be (more or less) quantified, and the company's attitude to new risk can, in principle, be dealt with simply and effectively. The acceptance of risk will be related to the size and robustness of opportunities open to the businesses.

How can risk be fit into deliberations of correct R&D strategies? The chief technologist repeatedly referred to risk. Was it the same kind of risk that he and his divisional presidents and vice presidents will plan around?

In R&D, risk is a specific, quantifiable dimension of planning used with a consistent meaning and set of implications. The CEO is not confident, however, that his general business managers are as rigorous in their use of the term. "A first principle of good planning is good communication," he says to the empty office. "And good communication demands that we all adhere to a common language with commonly accepted meaning and import." He reckons that a clarification of the terms *risk* and *uncertainty* for all his executives is necessary and makes a note to himself to call a meeting for this to occur.

He writes out the definition of *risk* henceforth to be expressed in his company: Risk = f(uncertainty ⟨or probability⟩ and exposure).

The magnitude of the risks acceptable to Intercontinental will be specific to the nature of the corporation and its businesses, to the industries in which the five divisions compete, and, of course, to the size and quality of the potential reward expected to be achieved if the outcome is successful. The relationship of acceptable risk to the minimum potential reward is depicted in Figure 5-6.

There are no rigorous definitions of "low," "moderate," or "high" risk or potential reward. Each is determined by the specifics of company culture, strategies, the industries in which the firm operates and by competitive conditions. For example, for an ethical pharmaceutical company, working at the frontiers of anticancer sciences,

Figure 5-6

The desired relationship between risk and reward in R&D investments

		Low	Moderate	High
Potential Reward	High	Excellent R&D Investment	Good-Excellent R&D Investment	(Possibly) Good-Excellent R&D Investment
	Moderate	Good R&D Investment	Acceptable-Good R&D Investment	
	Low	Acceptable R&D Investment		

Risk
(a function of the probability of success and financial exposure)

a moderate probability of success might be 20 percent. For a company in the business of developing a new line of cosmetics, a moderate probability of success might be 80 percent.

The CEO turns to Haber's three-year marketing and sales plan—familiar territory because the CEO cut his teeth in these areas of business.

The CEO is convinced that strategic planning for Intercontinental is based on one implicit assumption, that management must proactively address the question of the permanent survival of an enterprise. Management must look at the business, look at the external environment in which it is and will be operating, and initiate whatever changes are necessary to ensure the continuing profitability and survival of the business—indefinitely. Since technology is the single greatest source of change, it perforce becomes a central feature of strategic planning.

Strategic planning thus provides a doorway for R&D management to become more involved in the basic policy decisions of senior management.[3] The doorway is symbolically open. How many managers concerned with R&D and technology issues—and the integration of those issues into the business and corporate plans—pass through it is one measure of whether the organization is in a first, second, or third generation mode of R&D planning.

There follows for the CEO days of reviews; meetings on urgent marketing decisions, on a few regulatory issues, on a loan refinancing matter, and on organizational shuffles; an interview with *The Financial Times;* a crucial meeting with union leaders; and a couple of ceremonial appearances before employee groups. All of these activities keep the CEO from his paramount task—leading Intercontinental to distinction. He is almost relieved, however. The perfectly respectable, time-honored, full-calendar demands on his time are welcome. Circumstances remove him from the pressing demands of leadership and the planning that leadership demands.

More than a few CEOs have managed their companies by following a calendar of activities decided largely by others. Doing so is a seductive alternative to thinking, planning, proactivity, and leadership. Despite the sense of importance and personal comfort that the crowded calendar provides him, however, the CEO knows that a calendar dictated by immediate need is a tyranny.

He prevails over that tyranny and calls a meeting of all division presidents, their chief executives, and, explicitly, their vice presidents of R&D. The agenda is to develop a common vocabulary for planning, notably R&D planning, and to get a description by the CTO of the distinction between uncertainty and risk in both business and R&D plans and suggestions about how uncertainty can be transformed into risk for planning purposes.

Attendance at the CEO's meeting is complete though reluctant. After the CEO's introduction and admonitions, the chief technology officer begins.

"Let's pretend we can define a technological quality called the 'state of the art' with reference to a specific scientific or engineering field like, for example, understanding the genetics of the cocoa tree. We'll represent state-of-the-art knowledge symbolically on this chart [see Figure 5-7]. Everything below the line is within the state of the art; everything above is unexplored technological territory, dimensions unknown.

"If an R&D objective can be satisfied by knowledge within the state of the art, we can be reasonably confident of success because we are exploiting knowledge already in our heads. We'll still need creative skills, innovative talent, money, and energy, however, to

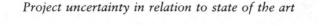

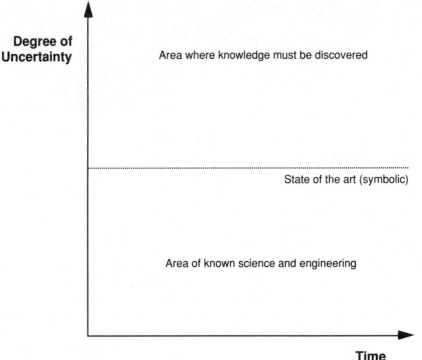

Source: Adapted from Philip A. Roussel, "Cutting Down the Guesswork in R&D," *Harvard Business Review* (September–October 1983), p. 157.

exploit that knowledge. But the technological risk—as distinct from the commercial risk, which is not my subject here—is rather low.

"Operating within the state of the art is roughly equivalent to what we call *incremental* R&D. *Radical* R&D, by definition, demands the development of knowledge that we, as a company, do not yet have. It is represented by the area near the symbolic boundary line labeled 'state of the art.' Others may have and apply that knowledge, and to them work in that technical area does not represent radical R&D. But if we do not possess it and must apply resources and time to develop it, it is radical R&D to us. I've illustrated that on another chart [see Figure 5-8].

"If our R&D target is at point A, somewhat distant from the most advanced technical frontier, the work will typically involve little technical risk; we can be 80 or 90 percent sure of success.

Figure 5-8

Project uncertainty in relation to state of the art, continued

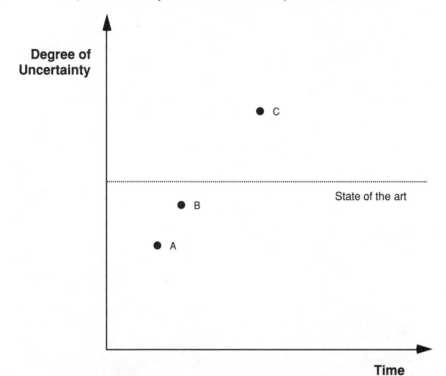

Source: Adapted from Philip A. Roussel, "Cutting Down the Guesswork in R&D," *Harvard Business Review* (September–October 1983), p. 157.

"If the target is at point B, closer to the frontier, the technical risk increases but not greatly; the probability of success may still be 70 to 80 percent.

"But once we cross the state-of-the-art boundary, it becomes impossible to predict with confidence the probability of reaching point C, when it might be accomplished, or how much effort it will take."

The CEO's focus on the charts is intense. "Let me restate what I think you're driving at. Below the line—within the state of the art—R&D results are more or less predictable. Given time, money, and creativity, we can reach almost any objective. A short distance above the boundary line represents radical R&D, and a greater distance above represents fundamental R&D."

"In symbolic terms, yes," says the chief technologist. "In this entire region above the state-of-the-art boundary, we are confronted with technological uncertainty.

"We all agree that as business people, we don't cope well with uncertainty. And so we undertake to transform uncertainty into risk. This is not easily done, but I'll try to explain how it is done.

"If research is trying to reach point C, in the region outside the boundary of the state of the art, it doesn't simply wander around, groping aimlessly, hoping that R&D will stumble across the solution. Almost always, a researcher will reason his or her way from what is known to a hypothesis about, or a theory about, what is unknown.

"For example, in the cocoa butter project being researched by Central Research, we have reasoned from studies of the molecular genetics of other species—call it biotechnology—that experimental techniques exist that will enable us to locate and identify the key genes of interest to us in the cocoa plant. We reason, and we postulate, that we can do it, using more or less established experimental approaches.

"So, we have a postulate whose truth or falsity is critical to success. We can estimate with reasonable confidence that the probability that we can successfully test the postulate is high—say, 60 to 70 percent. That test may take five or six man-years of work over a period of a year or two."

The CEO cuts in: "Sixty to 70 percent seems incredible for success in fundamental research. Isn't that what you've been preaching to me?"

"It is not a 60 to 70 percent chance of success for the project, only for a true/false test of the validity of the idea that is the project's foundation. This test determines only whether our foundation is solid or soft; it provides a go/no-go decision point that makes the project's overall uncertainty manageable."

"Is that like seeing the next card in stud poker before you decide to bet or fold?" the CEO asks, to some chuckles from the other executives.

"Close enough," the CTO says.

"Now, the cocoa butter project, if we are lucky enough to take it to completion, will take many millions of dollars and many years. Today we can assess potential reward, but we cannot truly assess the risk of getting it. So the risk/reward relationship is unknowable, or at least highly uncertain.

"But for $1 million or $2 million, we can do the exploratory work, the feasibility study if you will, the results of which will give

Figure 5-9

Project costs, cocoa butter example

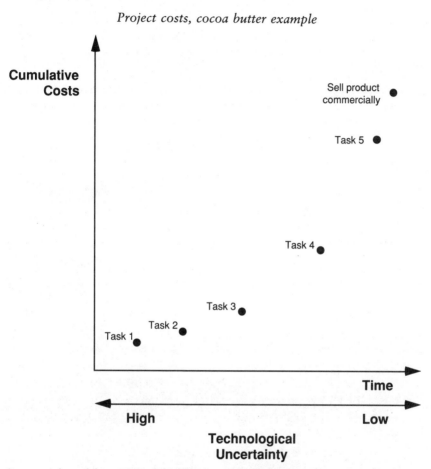

Source: Adapted from Philip A. Roussel, "Cutting Down the Guesswork in R&D," *Harvard Business Review* (September–October 1983), p. 159.

us pretty clear direction: stop the work or proceed. That, of course, is oversimplified. We must acknowledge some likelihood that the results from the exploratory phase will be inconclusive.

"Staying with the cocoa butter project, let's break down the costs, risks, and rewards from a business perspective—a strategic perspective—this way," the technologist says, flipping over another chart (see Figure 5-9).

"You don't move up the cumulative cost curve unless the results at task 1 are satisfactory. And satisfactory means that completion of the task reduces technological uncertainty. Graphically, the goal of each R&D task is to move as far toward the right on the horizontal axis—reducing technological uncertainty—for as little movement up the vertical axis—cumulative cost—as possible.

The CEO speaks again. "What you're saying is that you, the R&D manager, should never ask me, the general business manager, to underwrite a long-term project with very high uncertainty but no foreseeable costs over an indeterminate time. Or at least I should never let you do that. Instead, we should work out a plan where you ask me for increments of money with risk and time assessments—milestones—attached. I get multiple chances to bet or withdraw, depending on the results."

"Precisely. And I'm glad you said that you have a responsibility in this exercise. Far too often CEOs do almost nothing to evaluate this work, despite its long-term financial and strategic implications, because the early phases of the work cost relatively little and thus don't engage their attention. Look at the next graphic [see Figure 5-10], from the work of Edward Roberts.[4]

"Note that in a typical major project the real costs are not in the exploratory phase or in phases where uncertainties are highest; they are in the development or initial application phase, where costs really soar through the roof but where uncertainty—now expressed as risk—has been reduced to solid, businesslike proportions. Unfortunately, the typical CEO does not get interested in a project until he can have little impact on its eventual outcome, or until canceling it will entail a lot of wasted money.

"After looking at this, I hope all of you, Mr. CEO and division presidents, appreciate that you need to be atypical executives in order for Intercontinental to be truly prosperous."

The CEO chimes in again: "I wonder if there is an analogy here to test-marketing a new consumer product before investing the huge sums in advertising and promotion necessary to take the product national. That is, you need to reduce uncertainty at point X or Y before deciding to spend stratospheric sums up the vertical part of the curve."

"I had not ever thought of it in those terms," replies the chief technologist. "But there are parallels to be sure."

"I have a luncheon appointment soon," the CEO says, glancing at his watch. "Can we wrap this up by noon?"

"Certainly. I have only three more quick points. We can expand on them at another time if you like.

Figure 5-10

The typical role of the CEO in new product programs

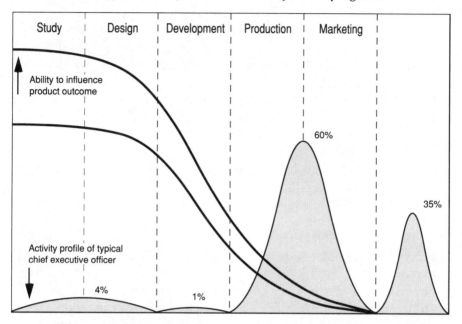

"The expertise of a chief executive can most influence any new technology-based product development program in the program's early stages – during preliminary study, design, and development. But current research suggests to the author that chief executive officers actually devote only trivial amounts of their time and attention to these early stages of such new-product programs. Instead, they typically have significant involvement only during production and marketing – when 'it's too late to do anything that can influence the outcome.'"

Source: Edward B. Roberts, "Generating Effective Corporate Innovation," *Technology Review* (October–November 1977), p. 2.

"Point one: If you decide to invest in a project like cocoa butter to point X on the curve, you are implicitly committing yourself to substantial future investments if we meet each milestone successfully. That is, your agreement to spend a little money for the feasibility study is a statement that you are willing, in principle, to invest many millions of dollars over the life of a successful project, maybe or maybe not including capital investments. So, I caution you, don't start down the path lightly."

"Who would?" the CEO asks.

"Many CEOs. As you saw from the graph, they simply don't or won't spend the time to consider projects like this one until big money is at stake, and that is usually late in the project.

"Point two: Divisions like Medelectronics almost certainly should not support fundamental research—they can't compete with the fundamental electronics technology giants around the world. And maybe the division should not even do any radical R&D. Look at the basis of competition, and you'll see entirely different demands for a division like Medelectronics and a division like Haber.

"Finally, point three . . ."

The CEO cuts in: "Like any good investment portfolio, balance is critical." He turns to the audience of divisional executives and asks, "Any comments?"

There are none. The CEO thinks for a moment, then again turns to his audience.

"If it's agreeable with you, I will charge our chief technology officer here with the responsibility to put these concepts into a form that we can take action on. Remember, the actions taken will undoubtedly place new work on your plates. I suggest you all go back and read that briefing paper I have enclosed in your notebooks."

Notes

1. Donald A. Schon, "The Fear of Science and Technology," in *Uncertainty in Research, Management, and New Product Development,* edited by R. M. Hainer, S. Kingsbury, and D. B. Gleicher (New York: Reinhold, 1967), p. 12.
2. Ibid.
3. Lowell W. Steele, "Selecting R&D Programs and Objectives," *Research & Technology Management,* vol. 31, no. 2 (March-April 1988), p. 17.
4. Edward B. Roberts, "Generating Effective Corporate Innovation," *Technology Review* (October-November 1977), pp. 27–33.

Briefing Paper 2

Technological Competitive Position

Managing technology strategically means doing three things right:

1. Recognizing important technologies for the business and the corporation—by their maturities and by their competitive impact
2. Mastering these important technologies to gain sustainable competitive advantage
3. Using these technologies effectively by integrating them with the other success factors of the business

In Briefing Paper 1 we discussed the concepts of technology maturity and competitive impact. Technology maturity places a technology along a continuum and helps one understand the possibilities for additional advances in the technology. Competitive impact of a technology is an indicator of the difference such additional advances make for the business. Both of these concepts apply in principle to all competitors in a particular business.

In this briefing paper we develop a third concept in managing technology strategically, that of technological competitive position, which measures the ability of a particular company to gain sustainable competitive advantage through technology and R&D in competition with other companies' R&D working toward the same objective.

In third generation management there is an ongoing effort to estimate the strengths of competitors in technologies important for the business and, where these are different, in technologies critical to the successful conduct of R&D. Technological competitive strength in the business is a measure of the degree to which a company masters important technologies relative to its competitors.

Although there are no rigorous measures of technological competitive strength, good technical judgments and insights are sufficient to make defensible estimates based on characteristics such as those

Figure Briefing 2-1

Generalized template for determining technological competitive strength

Descriptor	Characteristics
Dominant	• Powerful technological leader • High commitment, funds, manpower, creativity • Well recognized in industry • Sets pace and direction for technological development • Competitors consistently seek to catch up
Strong	• Able to express independent technical action, set new directions • Technological commitment and effectiveness consistently high • Technological accomplishments distinguish its strategic business units (SBU) from lesser competitors'
Favorable	• Able to sustain the technological competitiveness of the SBU it serves • Has strengths that can be exploited to improve technological competitive position • Not a technological leader except in developing niches
Tenable	• In a catch-up mode • Unable to set independent course • Can maintain competitiveness of SBU, but unable to differentiate it from competitors'
Weak	• Declining quality of technical output versus competitors • Short-term, firefighting focus • Products, processes, costs slipping relative to competitors' • Difficult but not impossible to turn around

shown in Figure Briefing 2-1. These estimates can be used to assess the R&D strengths of a company relative to those of competitors known or believed to be working in R&D toward the same objectives as one's own organization. In this context, technological competitive position is an expression of the size and competence of the resources an R&D organization can bring to bear to achieve a desired result.

Consider, for example, an R&D organization in only a "tenable" technological competitive position with reference to a project it considers undertaking. In the absence of strong mitigating circumstances, initiating the work would be distinctly unwise if the organization has estimated that one or two R&D competitors occupy strong technological competitive positions working toward the same objective. In that instance, the choice of the R&D planners is to reinforce the effort to bring it at least to parity with the strength of competitors or to abandon the project. There is little middle ground.

The maturity of critical R&D technologies has a bearing on the choice. If the technology is still in the embryonic stage, usually characterized by few participants and small resource commitments, a weak company may hope to catch up by increasing the size and quality of resources. If, on the other hand, the technology is well into the growth or mature stage, usually characterized by more participants and substantial resources, playing catch-up may be too costly and risky.

But even worse than undertaking an R&D objective from an inferior technological position in the face of known strong R&D competitors is undertaking the work in ignorance of competitors' technological competitive position. In such a situation, the R&D organization in the tenable position will lose the contest and waste resources and time it could have saved if it had analyzed its and its competitors' technological competitive position. A company that assigns three engineers to develop a new etching process for the manufacture of electronic circuits on a silicon chip is not likely to fare well against a competitor that undertakes the same project with fifty engineers.

Third generation companies use technology maturity and competitive position in R&D as an instrument of policy. Even small, innovation-driven biotechnology companies simply will not conduct R&D in areas where the technologies have already matured: "No me-too R&D for us," they say.

Larger pharmaceutical companies will conduct R&D with mature technologies only if they are at least strong relative to competitors: "The danger of coming in third or worse is too great," they say.

And companies that manufacture and compete on discrete new products will use only "proven technologies," meaning technologies that are well into the growth or mature stage, that they are confident they have mastered well enough to have a reasonable chance of getting into the market first.

It is not an accident that companies such as Fuji in consumer photographic film, Du Pont in medical X-ray systems, GE in certain engineering plastics, Toyota in automotive engines, and NEC in VCR systems are strong in the marketplace. By reputation, their business strategies call for leadership in those markets.

Leadership requires excellence in all functions that contribute to success, certainly including R&D. And in R&D excellence demands clear market vision, knowledge of competitors' technological strengths and weaknesses, and the ability to assemble and focus the R&D resources to place a business in a strong technological position, well at the forefront of the appropriate product and manufacturing technologies.

The need to apply these concepts is as evident for small companies as for the powerhouses cited above. For small companies, focusing to establish sufficient strength to outperform competitors may be even more compelling, although we are not aware of comparative studies that support such speculation. One can postulate that the successes of many small, startup high-tech companies is due in part to an almost single-minded dedication of R&D strength to a single technical area, focused on a single business opportunity.

A favorable-to-strong technological competitive position in R&D is a general precondition for competitiveness. In essence, it amounts to concentrating resources and focusing them where they can have the most competitive impact. Applying this precept inevitably demands difficult, even painful, choices between projects competing for limited resources.

In a creative R&D organization, attractive R&D concepts will always exceed the resources available for productive support. The temptation within management to support the creative ideas of an R&D organization's creative people is strong. It is difficult for most R&D managers to say to a researcher, in effect: "This is an attractive R&D concept, but if we proceed with it we will dilute the resources we can dedicate to other projects that we have decided are strategically more important."

R&D and business executives constantly face a paradox: how to maintain the intellectual vitality and creativity of an R&D organization while denying resources for intellectually attractive ideas in favor of strategically more important alternatives. It is common to find R&D executives who cannot bring themselves to say "no" to the ideas of respected researchers, even at the cost of technological competitive position in other work.

No paradox is easily resolved. In this situation, it is best dealt with by clear respect for the researcher and his ideas, at the same time bringing that researcher into the thinking and planning process where the focus of resources is determined.

As with all guidelines, there must be room for exceptions. If there are appropriate resources to provide strength to the major, strategically correct projects, it is often permissible and sometimes desirable to support exploratory or feasibility studies with modest funding and people. In these instances, the concept of technological competitive position loses much of its meaning. The lone explorer may be competing with no more than his or her own intellect. If the explorer is smart enough and lucky enough to find the object of the exploration—the success that commands technological and business exploitation—then the organization of that work must invoke the principle of technological competitive position.

For instance, the lone researcher's discovery of the sweetener aspartame had to be followed by decisions to make enormous, focused investments in development and exploitation.

In short, the evaluation of technological competitive position is a vital, if often neglected, tool of effective R&D planning. The company and its R&D organization(s) that apply the concept effectively will always possess significant advantages over companies that do not.

Chapter 6

The R&D Portfolio

The concept of business portfolios and the strategic options appropriate to developing and optimizing them began taking shape in the 1960s and became a powerful and pervasive planning tool in the 1970s. Because it has proved itself of great value, this concept—since extended to product portfolios—is well established and respected by senior executives in the United States, Western Europe, and Japan.

This chapter pushes the concept of business/product portfolios further, to the associated but somewhat different notion of the R&D portfolio, understood and applied even in 1990 by few of the world's most sophisticated companies. We anticipate that R&D portfolio analysis and planning will grow in the 1990s to become the powerful tool that business portfolio planning became in the 1970s and 1980s.

The purpose of both business and R&D portfolio planning typically is to reach the optimum point between risk and reward, stability and growth. The definition of *optimum,* of course, varies as widely as the ambitions, competence, vision, and culture of individual companies. To use the analogy of a sailboat, one skipper will trade off speed for comfort; another will yield comfort and even safety to acquire maximum speed; some will consider the "optimum" to be a balance of speed, comfort, and safety. Naturally, a company's R&D portfolio balance must be both developed and managed to support the overall business strategy.

Investment management provides another practical analogy. The effective investment manager must first help the client clarify and select appropriate investment goals: stable income, security, accumulated wealth, or a balance of all. Then, the investment manager must determine which investment vehicles, in combination, will realize the client's goals. The investment adviser builds a portfolio of investments that have the best chance of accomplishing the goals within risk constraints acceptable to the client. The adviser seeks balance among the investment characteristics of current yield, capital appreciation, and tax benefits and attempts to manage risk through

93

diversification. The investment program needs to be well executed and modified as conditions dictate, and its results need to be measured and reported to the client.

The R&D portfolio is made and managed in similar fashion. In this chapter we examine the nature of the R&D portfolio, both at a business level and for the corporation as a whole. We develop the theme of the strategic power of the R&D portfolio, explaining how it can multiply the effectiveness of R&D, reinforce the confidence of management, and help inspire the R&D organization(s) to higher levels of profitable productivity.

In third generation R&D management the development of the overall strategic plan—which includes the R&D plan—is an iterative process, with significant technical input from all levels of R&D and a great deal of give-and-take between business leadership, marketing, operations, and R&D. Strategic planning is greatly facilitated by the establishment of a common vocabulary among participants that ensures rigorous use of certain terms, expressions, and concepts: risk, uncertainty, technological maturity, competitive impact of technologies, technological competitive strength, and the strategic and operational distinctions between incremental, radical, and fundamental R&D.

To build up the R&D portfolio, business managers and R&D managers first examine each proposed individual project, then place each project within portfolio structures that accommodate the strategic elements most critical to the specific company and its industry. Individual projects are evaluated in terms of four key elements (earlier chapters introduced the first three of them):

- Technological competitive strength (i.e., how strong in R&D is a company compared with competitors believed to be pursuing the same objectives?)
- Technology maturity (i.e., how much possibility of technical advance remains in the key or pacing technologies embodied in the R&D projects?)
- Competitive impact of technologies (base, key, and pacing)
- R&D project attractiveness

The specific elements of project attractiveness and the importance of each element are situation-dependent. It is possible, however, to generalize about these elements for most companies in most industries (see Figure 6-1).

The first element of attractiveness—fit of the R&D project with

Figure 6-1

Typical elements of project attractiveness

Elements of R&D Project Attractiveness	Units in Which Attractiveness Is Expressed
Fit with business or corporate strategy	• A judgment ranging from **excellent to poor**
Inventive merit and strategic importance to the business	• The potential power of the sought-after result to: a) improve the competitive position of the business b) be applicable to more than one business c) provide the foundation for new businesses • A judgment from **high to low**
Durability of the competitive advantage sought	• **Years.** If the R&D result can be quickly and easily initiated by competitors, the project is less attractive than one that provides a protected, long-term advantage
Reward	• Usually financial, but sometimes "necessity work" (e.g., satisfying regulatory bodies) or building a knowledge base that becomes the foundation for applied work
Competitive impact of technologies	• **Base, key, pacing, embryonic.** If a project is made up entirely of the application of base technologies, it is classified as "base"; if a project contains at least one key or pacing technology, the entire project is classified as "key" or "pacing"
Uncertainty	
Probability of technical success	• Probability units, **0.1 - 0.9.** The probability that the objective will be achieved as defined
Probability of commercial success	• Probability units, **0.1 - 0.9.** The probability of commercial success if the project is technically successful
Probability of overall success	• Probability units, **0.1 - 0.9.** The product of technical and commercial probabilities
Exposure	
R&D costs to completion or key decision point	• **Dollars**
Time-to-completion or key decision point	• **Time**
Capital and/or marketing investment required to exploit technical success	• **Dollars**

business or corporate strategy—is a decisive one for all companies. If the fit is good to excellent, the remaining criteria come into consideration. If the fit is poor, the R&D project must be rejected outright or the strategy must be rethought.

As obvious as this fundamental test of attractiveness is, R&D and other senior managers often fail to ask the question. Even when they ask, they often fail to apply even the rudiments of sound strategic thinking and challenge to the answer. This lapse is not as astonishing as it seems. R&D organizations are populated by highly trained technical people, by nature creative and optimistic, to whom, in the absence of effective strategic leadership, the excitement of the technical challenge may be more important than the relevance of research results to business purposes. To this kind of person, the hunt is more exciting than the kill.

Fortunately, good management can lead that type of exploring mind to find excitement in technical work that is strategically relevant. It is rarely more difficult than making the strategy clear and making emphatic the importance of every individual R&D person and project to fulfilling the strategy.

If an individual R&D project passes the fundamental test of strategic relevance, the other criteria of attractiveness come into play.

Not all attractiveness criteria will be equally important. To some companies the time-to-completion of a project will be substantially more important than the durability of the technical success achieved by the work. Or the inventive merit will be more significant than the cost-to-completion. Typically, each criterion will be weighted—say, from one (least important) to five (most important)—with the weights decided by the particularities of the business and the industry in which it competes. A simple scoring system can then be applied to give a rough ranking of the attractiveness of projects under consideration (see Figure 6-2).

The criteria that decide project attractiveness may be used collectively or as individual components of portfolio consideration. Typically, individual criteria such as cost, probability of success, time-to-completion, and competitive impact will be considered in the aggregate estimation of project attractiveness and as significant individual variables in the portfolio evaluation, as they are later in this chapter.

The evaluation of project attractiveness in these terms is simple and reveals a great deal more than the scoring system suggests. It is simple because informed judgments rather than precision—based, say, on net present value calculations—provide the answers. The

Figure 6-2

Scoring individual projects for attractiveness

Illustrative Project

Criteria	Weight (1-5)	Rating (fit with criteria) (1-5)	Score (weight x rating)
Inventive merit (platform for expansion)	3	5	15
Durability of competitive advantage	5	3	15
Reward	5	4	20
Probability of technical success	2	2	4
Probability of commercial success	5	4	20
R&D costs to completion or key decision point	3	4	12
Time-to-completion or key decision point	2	4	8
Capital and/or marketing	1	3	3
TOTAL			97

Note: The overall score for this one project is 97 of a possible 130 or 75%.

literature is full of examples of the effectiveness of collective judgment in making such assessments.

Although some companies try to impose net present value (NPV) or discounted cash-flow (DCF) calculations, the range of uncertainties for research reaching out more than a year or two is so substantial that the rigor implied by NPV or DCF considerations becomes not only meaningless but possibly harmful.

Evaluation by these criteria reveals even more than the scoring system suggests because it identifies project strengths and weaknesses and forces management to consider questions such as these:

- If a project is estimated to take an excessively long time to complete, why?
- If that project is otherwise attractive, is there any action we can take to reduce the time-to-completion?
- Should we, for example, add more resources, or should we seek

to purchase elements of the technology in which we are not expert?

Further, such a simple, judgmental evaluation will force management to consider explicitly the full risk/reward relationships. It is easy enough for busy management to appropriate, say, $250,000 for a year of a project whose objective has a good ring to it. But a structured evaluation of the attractiveness of the project might reveal that the $250,000 is only a down payment on a cost-to-completion of $3–5 million, which, if successful, might require another $30 million to exploit.

Does such a project remain attractive?

Portfolio planning at the divisional level in the Haber Food Ingredients Division of Intercontinental proceeds with the assumption that company executives—top management, marketing, manufacturing, planning, and R&D executives—have safely if painfully negotiated the course of planning the five-year future of the business (or company) and have arrived at a general consensus on strategic direction and, at least in broad terms, the contribution that each function must make to fulfilling strategic goals.

The business strategies of the division have been established. As a first step, R&D has offered characterizations of the individual R&D projects that will support and enhance the probability of satisfying the overall strategic direction of the business. R&D, with participation by its clients in marketing, manufacturing, and general management, has evaluated these individual projects. Business and supporting R&D thrusts are outlined in Figure 6-3.

Now the individual projects are placed in the context of the portfolio variables that are key to the elements of balance that are appropriate for the division. The process can be likened to a funnel whose mouth is very wide to encourage the greatest creativity in idea generation and gestation but subjects the idea to a series of increasingly demanding screens to enhance the probability that the ideas that emerge from the screening are the most likely to serve the business strategy most effectively.

Conceptually, the presentation of a funnel is correct. But between concept and practice there is a large gulf over which at least two steps must be taken:

1. Each reasonable R&D project must be characterized in the terms described above.
2. All of the R&D projects must be assembled into portfolio

Figure 6-3

Haber Food Ingredients Division—general business strategies and proposed R&D thrusts

Business Cluster	Business Strategy	Proposed R&D Strategic Thrusts and Projects
Commodity ingredients	• Vanillin: achieve cost leadership; increase market share • Citric acid: maintain as service to customers	• Thrust: become lowest-cost producer of vanillin • Projects: develop improved manufacturing process – target cost reductions of 35%

Flavor extracts	• Expand by additions to current product line	• Thrust: exploit superior organoleptic skills to develop new products
		• Projects:
		  – Flavor extract of cola
		  – Flavor extract of syrups: maple, raspberry, blueberry

Natural flavor essences	• Maintain excellence of essences of butter and cheese • Expand by development of new, proprietary natural flavor essences	• Thrust: maintain technical leadership in natural flavor essence • Projects: develop natural flavor essences of beef, shrimp, salmon, lobster, crab
Sweetane; enzymes	• Expand by intensified marketing, sales, and service • Accelerate Enzyme Beta for production of noncaloric fat substitute	• Thrust: develop next generation of unique, proprietary, high-value products • Project: accelerate Enzyme Beta system for noncaloric fat production as rapidly as possible

New business ventures	• Diversify product portfolio within food-ingredients industry with proprietary, high-value-in-use products	• Thrust: diversify product portfolio within food-ingredients industry with proprietary, high-value-in-use products
		• Projects:
		  – Conduct fundamental research on genetics of the cocoa tree; determine feasibility of constructive modification of genes
		  – Initiate exploratory project for organic salt mimic to replace natural salt
		  – Initiate exploratory project to reduce manufacturing cost of Sweetane

All businesses	• Maintain superior capability and capacity in technical service to customers	• Maintain superior capability and capacity in technical service to customers

representations that evoke the right strategic and operational questions.

As the Haber executives ponder the proposed R&D thrusts and supporting projects, the chief technology officer introduces the concept of R&D portfolio balance.

"The elements or variables that should be considered in R&D portfolio balance are as numerous—given its resources—or as limited as a company needs them to be to fulfill its business strategies.

Figure 6-4

Haber Food Ingredients Division—R&D Portfolio Dimensions

Annual R&D project cost

R&D project cost to completion

Probability of success

Technological maturity

Technological competitive strength

Project attractiveness

Competitive impact of the technologies embedded in the project

Time-to-completion

For Haber, I believe the elements of balance we must consider are as follows."

The CTO produces the first of a series of charts (see Figure 6-4).

"Many of you have participated in the characterization of the individual projects proposed. My staff and I have taken those results and displayed them in several different portfolio contexts in ways that we believe will facilitate the decisions the division must make about what to fund, at what levels, and what not to fund.

"First, we will look at the proposed projects R&D has worked out with you to support your business thrusts. The next chart [see Figure 6-5] shows those individual projects and the budget distribution allotted to them within the proposed R&D budget guideline of $18 million. It also shows the level of spending that, in our judgment, would be required for timely completion of those projects. You will note a significant mismatch between the proposed allocations and the optimum ones of close to $5 million.

"Now we will look at the proposed projects in the first of several portfolio structures. In the first representation [see Figure 6-6], we depict for each proposed project our technological competitive position, the maturity of the relevant technologies embedded in each, and the recommended budget, symbolized by the area within the circles. The numbers in the circles identify the proposed projects.

Figure 6-5

Haber Food Ingredients Division—first R&D project proposal

Proposed Annual Budget

	PROJECT	Proposed by R&D ($ 000)		Optimum for Accelerated Results ($ 000)
1	Manufacturing cost – vanillin	$400		$700
2	Cola extract	$100		$200
3	Maple extract	$150	$550	$300
4	Raspberry extract	$150		$300
5	Blueberry extract	$150		$300
6	Beef natural essence	$300		$900
7	Shrimp natural essence	$400		$1,000
8	Salmon natural essence	$400	$1,900	$1,000
9	Lobster natural essence	$400		$1,100
10	Crab natural essence	$400		$1,100
11	Enzyme Beta (noncaloric fat substitute)	$2,000		$2,000
12	Salt mimic	$500		$500
13	Cost reduction – Sweetane	$600		$600
14	Fundamental (cocoa tree genetics)	$2,000		$2,000
15	Technical service to customers	$7,000		$7,000
16	Discretionary research	$500		$1,000
SUBTOTAL		**$15,450**		**$20,000**
Necessity R&D	Environmental control		$1,100	
	Quality assurance		$900	
	Legal, patents, and licensing		$300	
	Community and university support		$500	
TOTAL		**$18,250**		**$22,800**

Figure 6-6

Annual budget, technological competitive position, and technological maturity

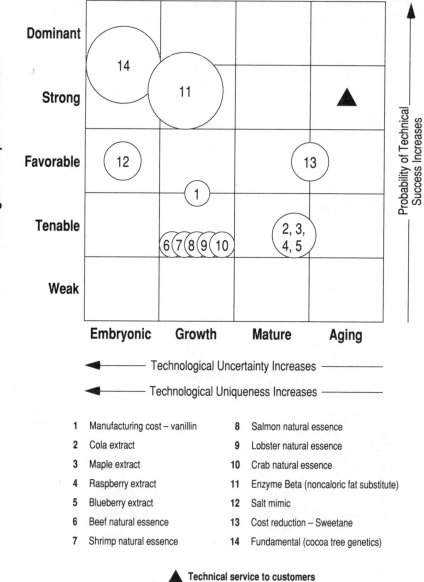

Haber R&D Portfolio as Originally Proposed

			Manufacturing cost – vanillin		Salmon natural essence

1   Manufacturing cost – vanillin   8   Salmon natural essence

2   Cola extract   9   Lobster natural essence

3   Maple extract   10 Crab natural essence

4   Raspberry extract   11 Enzyme Beta (noncaloric fat substitute)

5   Blueberry extract   12 Salt mimic

6   Beef natural essence   13 Cost reduction – Sweetane

7   Shrimp natural essence   14 Fundamental (cocoa tree genetics)

▲ Technical service to customers

"What does this display suggest? By itself, it is insufficient for decision making, but it raises some interesting questions.

"For instance, why are we in a low 'tenable' competitive position in projects 2 through 10? 'Tenable' is not a good place to be in R&D. Typically, that position means that results will not be timely and that our competitors may get to the same objectives before we do.

"Why are those projects in that position? Because we do not have the resources in money and people for that many projects in flavor extracts and natural flavor essences. What does that suggest to you?

"In contrast, we are extremely strong in the radical project for Enzyme Beta and in the fundamental project on the genetics of the cocoa tree. Why? Because in the recent past R&D has assembled very strong resources in technical sophistication, relevant experience, and manpower to address those two scientifically demanding projects.

"We are in acceptable competitive positions on the projects for a salt mimic (12), vanillin cost reduction (1), and Sweetane cost reduction (13), again determined by resource allocations.

"This portfolio display [Figure 6-6] also shows a concentration of a major part of our resources in the technically uncertain embryonic and growth technologies (setting aside, for this discussion, the $7 million in technical service to customers, which is technically highly certain). Thus two appropriate questions present themselves. First, is it prudent to place the bulk of our effort there? Second, does that represent good balance?

"The first representation does not answer these questions, but it certainly poses them in a compelling way. Now let's look at another portfolio representation.

"In the next display [see Figure 6-7], we are relating the annual budget for each project to the potential reward and to the overall probability of success, one component in the risk equation. Quantitative definitions of the meaning of 'modest reward,' 'outstanding reward,' etc., are given in your briefing notes. What questions arise now? I'll suggest some.

"Why is the reward low for flavor-extract projects 2 through 5 and the probability of overall success only about 70 percent?

"Answer: Because the judgment is that resources are too modest in these projects to get to the market before competitors do. Although the probability of technical success is high, the probability of commercial success is diminished because we will be late to market. Much of the same reasoning applies to flavor-essence projects 6

Figure 6-7

Potential reward and probability of overall success

Haber R&D Portfolio as Originally Proposed

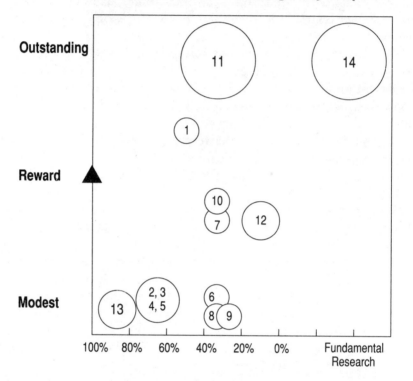

Probability of Overall Success
(probability of technical success x probability of commercial success)

1	Manufacturing cost – vanillin	**8**	Salmon natural essence
2	Cola extract	**9**	Lobster natural essence
3	Maple extract	**10**	Crab natural essence
4	Raspberry extract	**11**	Enzyme Beta (noncaloric fat substitute)
5	Blueberry extract	**12**	Salt mimic
6	Beef natural essence	**13**	Cost reduction – Sweetane
7	Shrimp natural essence	**14**	Fundamental (cocoa tree genetics)

▲ **Technical service to customers**

through 10, where technical success is more uncertain. Note, too, that the potential rewards for three of those projects are low. The question raised here is: Are the potential rewards commensurate with overall uncertainty?

"Surely project 13, cost reduction for Sweetane, will raise questions. The proposed budget for the project—$600,000—is large, and the reward is low. Should we fund it?

"And are there means to improve the probability of success of projects whose promise of reward is excellent but whose probability of success is only 30 to 50 percent? Is the very low probability of success for the salt mimic (project 12) congruent with our strategies and the projected reward?"

The CTO continues with several additional displays of the proposed R&D projects, each with a different analytical and strategic perspective.

"Ladies and gentlemen, you will tire of seeing the same projects displayed again and again in different structures; but please bear with me. No single display can possibly convey all of the complexities of the proposed portfolio."

Mindful that this is the first exposure of the Haber executives to R&D portfolio thinking, the CTO continues his presentation of portfolio variables and displays, cuing the audience with the key questions that each analytical representation should raise. He knows—and he has warned the CEO—that it will probably take two or three complete planning cycles before the questions—and their answers—become natural and spontaneous to the executives.

For completeness, he is compelled to show more than the impatient executives want to see. For both immediate and lasting effect, he has to provide sufficient analytical power for skeptical executives. And he wants to leave the audience with the conviction that their investment in time and energy has been worthwhile.

An abstracted version of the remainder of his presentation follows in Figures 6-8, 6-9, and 6-10. Each figure offers a new analytical and strategic representation of the proposed R&D portfolio and the new questions it raises.

Key Questions:

1. For Haber, is this an appropriate distribution of investment and time-to-completion?
2. Except for the $7 million in customer service, more than 90 percent of the R&D budget won't yield commercially usable

results for at least two to three years, and more than half of the projects have times-to-completion more than three years away. Is this sensible?

3. Can our kind of business stand the really long-term, high-cost R&D investments whose results are five or more years away?

Key Question:

1. For Haber, is this an appropriate distribution of R&D investment and competitive impact? Can a company this size afford so much investment in pacing technologies and the special risks they entail? Are there other, lower-cost options for pursuing these futures that would allow us to invest in, say, key technologies with profit impact in the nearer term?

Key Questions:

1. For Haber, is this an appropriate distribution of investment and the uncertainties associated with technologies and markets?
2. In particular, projects 11 (Enzyme B noncaloric fat substitute) and 12 (salt mimic) combine the dual uncertainties of technology and market. Are the heavy investments in them appropriate for Haber?
3. Is Haber doing enough in new technologies to reinforce its position in markets in which it is already a major player?

Are these good portfolios? In the abstract, no one can say. But surely even these simple depictions are certain to raise important questions in the executives' minds.

The following key strategic questions for management are suggested by Figures 6-8, 6-9, and 6-10:

- How important is R&D to the success of the business?
- If it is important, in what kinds of R&D should we invest? Should we invest in base, key, pacing, or embryonic technologies? In incremental, radical, or fundamental R&D?
- How do we assure the integration of R&D plans and business plans into one effective, overall strategic plan?
- In short, what is the optimum portfolio of R&D projects in the context of the short-, medium-, and long-term strategic needs of, and opportunities for, the division?

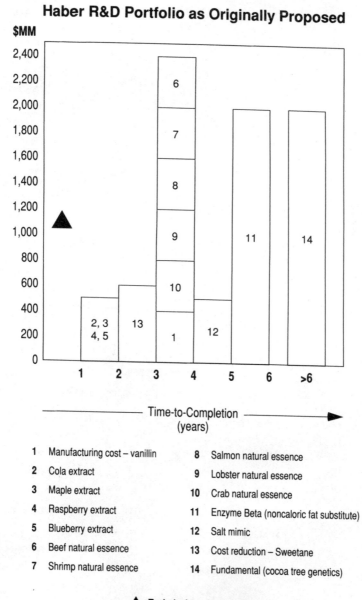

Figure 6-8

Annual budget and estimated time-to-completion

Haber R&D Portfolio as Originally Proposed

1   Manufacturing cost – vanillin   8   Salmon natural essence

2   Cola extract   9   Lobster natural essence

3   Maple extract   10   Crab natural essence

4   Raspberry extract   11   Enzyme Beta (noncaloric fat substitute)

5   Blueberry extract   12   Salt mimic

6   Beef natural essence   13   Cost reduction – Sweetane

7   Shrimp natural essence   14   Fundamental (cocoa tree genetics)

▲ Technical service to customers

Figure 6-9

Annual budget and competitive impact of technologies

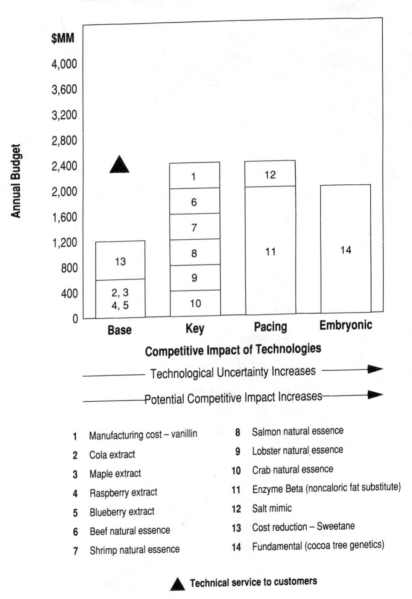

Haber R&D Portfolio as Originally Proposed

1   Manufacturing cost – vanillin
2   Cola extract
3   Maple extract
4   Raspberry extract
5   Blueberry extract
6   Beef natural essence
7   Shrimp natural essence

8   Salmon natural essence
9   Lobster natural essence
10 Crab natural essence
11 Enzyme Beta (noncaloric fat substitute)
12 Salt mimic
13 Cost reduction – Sweetane
14 Fundamental (cocoa tree genetics)

▲ Technical service to customers

Figure 6-10

Annual budget and familiarity of technologies and markets

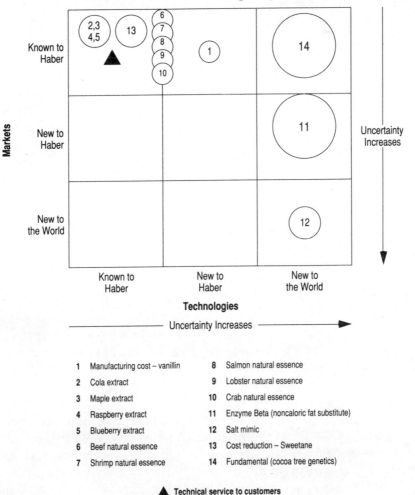

Haber R&D Portfolio as Originally Proposed

	1	Manufacturing cost – vanillin	8	Salmon natural essence
	2	Cola extract	9	Lobster natural essence
	3	Maple extract	10	Crab natural essence
	4	Raspberry extract	11	Enzyme Beta (noncaloric fat substitute)
	5	Blueberry extract	12	Salt mimic
	6	Beef natural essence	13	Cost reduction – Sweetane
	7	Shrimp natural essence	14	Fundamental (cocoa tree genetics)

▲ Technical service to customers

Let's now consider a single project (project 12) being evaluated for the Haber Food Ingredients Division. The provocative title of the project is "New Salt Substitutes for the Retail Market: Organic Salt Mimics to Replace Sodium Chloride."

A promising laboratory lead exists. The objective plays to a real consumer health need. Competitive products are poor. The Haber product could probably be protected by patents. The potential rewards are vast. Costs, at least to key decision points, are acceptable. The R&D organization is enthusiastic about chances of success. Yet the project scores low in overall attractiveness. The discussion between division and R&D management might go like this:

Division: This looks like a really hot prospect. Why does it score so low?

R&D: First, because it is only marginally consistent with our strategy of being a leading company in the food-ingredients industry. This is not a food ingredient. Its development would take us into the retail food industry, where we have no presence, no experience, and little understanding of the competitive dynamics. So the probability of commercial success is only modest. Second, salt mimics would almost certainly not be natural products and would therefore require FDA approval—we know that is a long and extremely costly process. Given the problems of uncertainty, time, and cost, and our resource constraints, we judge it to be relatively unattractive.

Division: Then what should we do?

R&D: We propose not to undertake the research ourselves but to offer—for a share of the profits—our research lead to a company that has the appropriate experience, strategy, and resources—like Procter & Gamble or Unilever.

Without the simple analysis of attractiveness, Haber might have been propelled by R&D's enthusiasm into funding this tantalizing project, without recognizing the strategic, competitive, regulatory, and cost pitfalls associated with it.

An alternative scenario for an R&D project in Haber, with the title "An Improved Manufacturing Process for Vanillin: Potential Cost Reduction of 35 Percent," whose attractiveness score was also low, might go like this:

Division: This is a cost-based business. Thirty-five percent is terrific. Why does this project score so low?

R&D: For two reasons. First, with the technical resources we can deploy, the work might take three or four years to complete. We think a Japanese company is working toward the same end and that it might get

	there before us. Second, we lack certain technical capabilities, notably in phase transfer catalysis and membrane separations.
Division:	What happens if you add those resources?
R&D:	We have considered that and have determined that we can add them, at an incremental cost of about $300,000 per year, improve the probability of success, and reduce the time-to-completion to perhaps one or two years.

These examples should provide sufficient reason to undertake judgmental evaluations of R&D projects according to criteria of attractiveness. But there are other reasons.

In any strategically well-managed R&D organization, there will be and should be more project concepts than the company can afford to undertake. In first generation R&D management, the decision about which projects to fund and which to shelve or postpone is left largely to the judgment of R&D management, governed by the size of the annual budget rather than by a robust strategic context.

But in third generation R&D planning, R&D needs to offer business executives more projects than can reasonably be funded. That need not only forces compelling questions but offers executives a choice of the best assembly of projects for the short-, medium-, and long-term health of the business.

With portfolio displays and accompanying discussions, the CTO feels that the executives have sufficient information to understand key dimensions of R&D portfolio balance and the key decisions Haber must make. In planning the review, he and the CEO agreed to conclude the presentation with the background analysis and the questions it stimulated, ask the executives to study the presentation overnight, and resume deliberations the next morning. At that time, the subject of discussion will be portfolio decisions that would guide the technology component of the business strategy for the future.

The CTO concludes the review with remarks both comforting and sobering.

"First, be comforted by the fact that this process looks more intimidating than it actually is because it is all new to you. In future planning cycles you will find this kind of thinking more natural, almost as natural as you now consider marketing directions and budgets.

"Second, all of this discussion treats our R&D portfolio planning as a zero-based budgeting assignment. In reality, each future planning cycle will see many of the same proposals before you, with perhaps 10 to 20 percent of the plan representing new projects. Although we must reconsider all of the projects, whether ongoing or newly proposed, in every plan 80 to 90 percent of them will already be familiar to you. The rate of technical progress will be known to you, assumptions will be clearer and surer, and your knowledge base will be stronger.

"That may ease the pain of this exercise a little, but there is a sobering side to it, with which the CEO will conclude this meeting."

The CEO rises and surveys the audience.

"This has been a demanding review. I am absolutely convinced of its value, and I want you to be as convinced as I am. As you do your homework this evening, keep in mind two points.

"First, contrast what you know about the role of R&D in our business with what you knew from the planning process when I first arrived. In those discussions, R&D was scarcely mentioned. You treated it more as an unavoidable nuisance than as a source of competitive strength.

"Second, remember that the decisions we will make about the R&D portfolio tomorrow will have major, lasting consequences on Haber's future performance. The consequences won't be for a quarter or a year, but for years.

"You must consider the cost involved, of course, but also the benefits, timing, competitive impact, uncertainty, and risk. You must consider that if we fund project X, we may not be able to afford to fund project Y. Conversely, you must ask yourself not only if we are spending well on the R&D portfolio, but whether our level of spending is too much or too little to serve our business strategies. You must search your business souls to identify possible new and better opportunities for R&D investment than those now before us. You must consider what our competitors are up to in their laboratories.

"In short, take this planning responsibility as seriously as I have come to take it. And prepare yourselves well for the decision-making meeting tomorrow."

The Outcome

The next day's meeting is characterized by debate, challenge, occasional confusion, dismay when pet projects come under attack, and occasional contentiousness. But the CEO and CTO see to it that the course is stayed, and by dinnertime the group has welded together an R&D portfolio plan that all agree could never have been attained under any previous planning process. The key decisions and part of their rationale are shown in Figure 6-11.

But the rationale expressed in Figure 6-11 is incomplete. It looks as if the senior executives had examined the constituent trees instead of the strategic forest. If this alone were the outcome, it would represent the evaluation of R&D work on a project-by-project basis, encouraging the executives to probe into technical details they are ill equipped to handle. Had the planning process ended with a project-by-project evaluation, it would have represented a classic example of second generation R&D planning.

But under the impulse of the new planning mode, all of the proposed work was placed in the strategic portfolio representations shown earlier (Figures 6-6, 6-7, 6-8, 6-9, and 6-10), and the decisions about which work to fund and at what level, and which ones not to fund, were made in the portfolio context.

Those decisions, in a portfolio structure, resolved many of the questions evoked by the strategic challenges of the portfolio matrices. Figure 6-12 displays the decisions to abandon flavor-extract projects 2 and 5 and flavor-essence projects 6, 8, and 9, in which Haber could participate only at a "tenable" competitive position, and concentrate instead on improving technological competitive position in flavor-extract projects 3 and 4 and flavor-essence projects 7 and 10. The resources taken from the rejected projects were added to the retained projects, supporting the option to improve Haber's technological competitive position in the retained projects from tenable to favorable or strong and, in constructive consequence, compressing the time to both project completion and market introduction.

Figure 6-13 reflects the same decisions in the matrix that expresses the relationship between potential reward, the probability of overall success of the work, and the size of the budgets allocated to each project. The improvements in those relationships are compelling.

The time to project completion is always a key competitive concern. Delay means that the future grows more uncertain because business and competitive uncertainty increase exponentially with time and because delay offers competitors the opportunity to achieve success first, possibly to pre-empt the market. The decisions reflected in Figure 6-14 show a marked improvement in the time component of the revised portfolio. By concentrating resources and, in the case of Enzyme Beta noncaloric fat substitute, forming a strategic alliance,

Figure 6-11

Haber R&D portfolio as revised

Project No.	Objective	Budget ($000) Original	Budget ($000) New	Rationale
1	Reduce manufacturing cost – Vanillin – up to 35%	$400	$700	• High return, shorten time-to-completion, reduce uncertainty, beat competition, improve project attractiveness
	Flavor Extracts			
2	Cola	$100	$0	• Omit cola – too competitive, no special place for Haber
3	Maple	$150	$300	• Expand maple and raspberry extract R&D, reduce time-to-completion, improve project attractiveness
4	Raspberry	$150	$300	
5	Blueberry	$150	$0	• Omit blueberry – market uncertainties
	Natural Flavor Essences			• Omit beef, salmon, and lobster – uncertain markets
6	Beef	$300	$0	
7	Shrimp	$400	$1,000	• Improve probability of success, improve project attractiveness for shrimp; reduce time-to-completion
8	Salmon	$400	$0	
9	Lobster	$400	$0	
10	Crab	$400	$1,000	• Improve probability of success, improve project attractiveness for crab; reduce time-to-completion
11	Enzyme Beta (low-calorie fat substitute)	$2,000	$1,000	• Form R&D joint venture with major food-oil products company (e.g., Unilever) • Reduce exposure, add technical know-how and marketing power of partner • Probably accelerate project
12	Develop organic salt mimic	$500	$0	• Avoid dual technical and commercial risk • Sell technology to major retail food company (e.g., Procter & Gamble, Kraft-General Foods) • Retain royalty rights • Reduce overall portfolio and business risk
13	Reduce Sweetane manufacturing cost	$600	$0	• Benefit not commensurate with cost • Improvements incremental only, not protectable
13A	Exploratory – radical research to reduce manufacturing cost of Sweetane	$0	$200	• Long-term strategy needed as Sweetane patent expires • If successful, major protectable cost reduction
14	Fundamental – cocoa tree genetics for improved cocoa butter yield	$2,000	$2,500	• Major, proprietary potential • Increase probability of success, reduce time by contract research and joint venture inducements with established plant R&D biotechnology company
15	Technical service to customers	$7,000	$7,000	• Essential to business sustainability and competitive position
16	Discretionary R&D	$500	$1,000	• Increase scope of search for new R&D ideas, expand funding of creative exploratory work
	Subtotal	$15,450	$15,000	
	Necessity R&D			
	Environmental control	1,100	1,100	
	Quality assurance	900	900	
	Legal, patents, licensing	300	300	
	Community/university support	500	700	
	TOTAL	**$18,250**	**$18,000**	

Figure 6-12

Improving technological competitive position in the Haber R&D portfolio

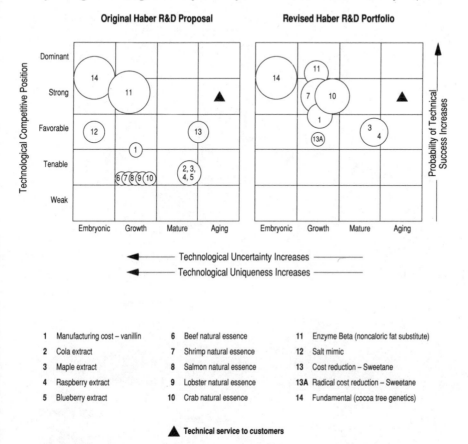

1	Manufacturing cost – vanillin	6	Beef natural essence	11	Enzyme Beta (noncaloric fat substitute)
2	Cola extract	7	Shrimp natural essence	12	Salt mimic
3	Maple extract	8	Salmon natural essence	13	Cost reduction – Sweetane
4	Raspberry extract	9	Lobster natural essence	13A	Radical cost reduction – Sweetane
5	Blueberry extract	10	Crab natural essence	14	Fundamental (cocoa tree genetics)

▲ Technical service to customers

the projected times-to-completion of all projects were compressed significantly. The competitive benefits are transparent.

Finally, the Haber executives made their R&D decisions around the elements of the familiarity index, electing to focus resources largely in markets well known to Haber, eliminating the salt-mimic project by the sale of the know-how already accumulated, and reducing their exposure in the Enzyme Beta project by forming an R&D partnership to share its costs. They did not eliminate all major risk. They retained the cocoa butter project, characterized by substantial technical risk, but, since Haber already participated in cocoa butter production and marketing, they avoided meaningful market risk. Those decisions are represented in Figure 6-15.

Figure 6-13

Enhancing the reward-uncertainty relationship

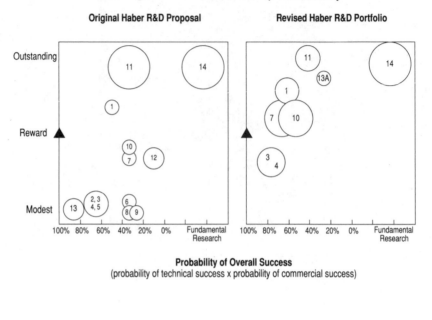

1	Manufacturing cost – vanillin	6	Beef natural essence	11	Enzyme Beta (noncaloric fat substitute)
2	Cola extract	7	Shrimp natural essence	12	Salt mimic
3	Maple extract	8	Salmon natural essence	13	Cost reduction – Sweetane
4	Raspberry extract	9	Lobster natural essence	13A	Radical cost reduction – Sweetane
5	Blueberry extract	10	Crab natural essence	14	Fundamental (cocoa tree genetics)

▲ Technical service to customers

These portfolio matrices are only tools. By themselves, they provide no answers. But they do help enforce a kind of strategic discipline. Properly and objectively constructed and displayed, properly involving the inputs from R&D, marketing, manufacturing, and senior management, they can lead to decisions virtually foreclosed by other planning methods.

In reaching its decisions, the management group can feel certain that it has caused meaningful, constructive, and powerful change in the R&D plans of the Haber Food Ingredients Division. The changes are powerful because they are strategic, because they were forced by considerations of the R&D component of business success never before contemplated.

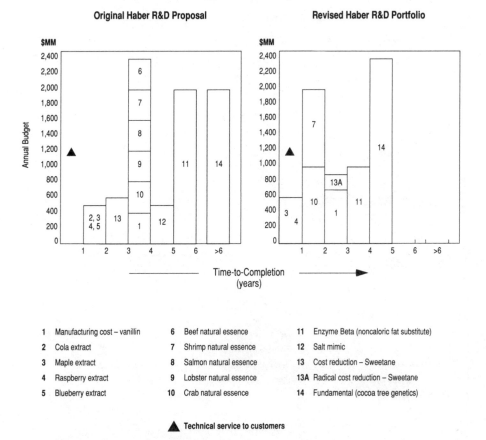

Figure 6-14

Shortening time-to-completion

1 Manufacturing cost – vanillin	6 Beef natural essence	11 Enzyme Beta (noncaloric fat substitute)
2 Cola extract	7 Shrimp natural essence	12 Salt mimic
3 Maple extract	8 Salmon natural essence	13 Cost reduction – Sweetane
4 Raspberry extract	9 Lobster natural essence	13A Radical cost reduction – Sweetane
5 Blueberry extract	10 Crab natural essence	14 Fundamental (cocoa tree genetics)

▲ Technical service to customers

The management group has forced rethinking the future. The managers have demanded focus. They have required the evaluation of competitors' R&D. They have forced a distinction between easy and superficially attractive incremental R&D and more aggressive work whose results, though less sure, are likely to have much greater impact on the business. They have forged a new level of understanding, confidence, and mutual trust among general management, marketing, sales, manufacturing, planning, and R&D. They have forged the beginning—surely only the beginning—of third generation R&D planning.

Not mentioned by the participants but recognized by the CEO and his CTO, the planning process, however painful and time-

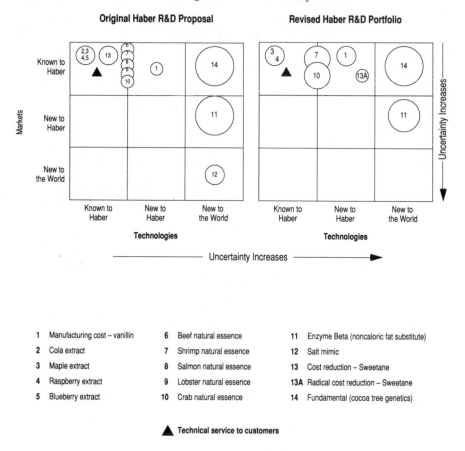

Figure 6-15

Reducing market uncertainty

1   Manufacturing cost – vanillin
2   Cola extract
3   Maple extract
4   Raspberry extract
5   Blueberry extract

6   Beef natural essence
7   Shrimp natural essence
8   Salmon natural essence
9   Lobster natural essence
10 Crab natural essence

11 Enzyme Beta (noncaloric fat substitute)
12 Salt mimic
13 Cost reduction – Sweetane
13A Radical cost reduction – Sweetane
14 Fundamental (cocoa tree genetics)

▲ Technical service to customers

consuming, has caused the adoption and use of a new, commonly understood, vocabulary, facilitating the exchanges.

For the first time, R&D was summoned to provide realistic estimates of what it can deliver in terms of cost, time, and results, all modified by uncertainty. For the first time, the business people responded to the demand for realistic estimates of competitors' action, market opportunities, and their own uncertainties about commercial potential. For the first time, general management became engaged at a depth that provided authority to the planning process and commitment to the plan.

But the CEO and CTO know that they have made only a start on a long journey. The CEO is reminded of Churchill's words when his embattled nation first seemed to have stayed the enemy's previously inexorable march: "This is not the end. It is not even the beginning of the end. But it is, perhaps, the end of the beginning."

The CEO and CTO are concerned that the participants were not fully objective, that bias crept into the process. Both wonder whether commitment will last through the inevitable bad times ahead or whether the predisposition to focus narrowly on function instead of on the prosperity of the division might return. Both are convinced that steps toward the vital goal of true partnership have been made, but the distance between functions still has not been fully closed. They both know that one planning exercise is not sufficient to change a culture. It is up to them to enforce through leadership the cultural change that will make the partnership endure.

"You know," says the CTO to his boss, "we've done a good job with the division. But you have five divisions. Not only must we go through similar planning with the other four, but then we must integrate the R&D plans of the five divisions for the best future of Intercontinental as a whole."

The CEO looks dismayed. "I recognize the need to apply this discipline to all divisions. But what is this integration process? I thought our total R&D plan would be the sum of the five divisions' plans."

"To a large extent it will be," the CTO says reassuringly. "But, just as you consider the allocation of funds for major capital investments from a corporate point of view, you must consider R&D investments corporately. Don't worry, it's not such a big job. My staff and I can prepare a background briefing to prepare you and the division executives to take the corporate view.

"I'll offer a simple example of the R&D issues we need to face corporately:

"Three of the divisions—Haber, Medelectronics, and Mason Seed—each have a significant R&D effort in biotechnology; the gene modification work you've heard about in Haber's plans is an example. The corporate decision will have to do with whether to consolidate the three divisions' biotech work.

"Why consolidate? Possibly for mutual reinforcement, for mutual scientific excitement and stimulation, to decide who will provide research leadership, even to decide how to fund such 'crossover' technologies in the future.

"It is important, but not so arduous. Mostly, the individual divisions' R&D plans will stand as if they were drawn up for individual companies. Corporately, we must look for cross-divisional synergies, conflicts, or duplications and make the appropriate organizational funding decisions.

"There is another consequence of this planning process we haven't discussed. You and I, by our participation and endorsement, have joined the accountability chain. This is not *their* plan for which we can point a finger in the case of problems. It is *our* plan. We can hold the businesses and R&D accountable for performance against the plan, for achieving milestones, for progress toward objectives, but not for the objectives or for the plan itself."

The CEO replies, "I think that is a great result as long as the plan is developed collectively, as it was, and agreed to by all, as it was.

"But there is something I don't know," the CEO pauses and gazes at his CTO. "I don't have the faintest idea how to hold R&D accountable. A business, sure. A business makes commitments for sales, costs, earnings, growth, capital investments and their return, and so on. All of those are measurable in units I understand—dollars, percentages, margins. How do I judge R&D, patents, new products introduced, cost reductions? How?"

"By none of those measures," the chief technologist replies. "To many executives, the subject of R&D accountability is a mystery. R&D tends to justify its work in the units you describe, plus technical reports that only technical people can evaluate. 'Look how brilliant we are,' these technical reports say; they cause more suspicion than enlightenment.

"You hold R&D accountable exactly as you hold a business—say, Haber—or a function of a business, such as manufacturing, accountable. By its performance with reference to commitments made in the plan. A business will commit itself to millions of dollars of sales per year at a certain gross-profit margin. A function like manufacturing will commit itself to a certain volume of production at certain costs, a certain level of produced quality, safety performance, assurance of safe environmental practices, and so on.

"R&D accountability is exactly the same. You or the business vice president measures the performance of R&D according to the commitments R&D has made in the plan. Those commitments may be expressed in units you are less comfortable with, but units you can still manage: arriving at milestones, reducing uncertainty, a new product introduction, a cost reduction on time, even in the murky realm of exploratory or fundamental R&D, whether the results support continuing the work, ending it, or just framing the questions more pointedly.

"Most studies on R&D accountability are simply wrong. They

try to measure the wrong things, usually retrospectively. The real, and the only, prospective measurables reside in the progress toward agreed-upon objectives. And the use of these measurables is effective only if the business leadership has participated in establishing the portfolio of objectives."

The CEO rises. "Let's end on a positive note. I can't prove it, but I project that we will find over time that the R&D people are as excited as I am. They will like being an integral part of strategy instead of a line-item cost. They will like their contribution measured realistically. They will like feeling that they are an important part of the enterprise instead of misunderstood adjuncts to it. And that, I believe, will all add up to productivity."

Chapter 7

Organizing R&D for Results

To this point, we have addressed the planning and strategic issues that a CEO and his management team should consider when planning R&D, identifying targets and setting priorities, and allocating resources. But the responsibility of senior management does not end there.

Primary responsibility for executing the plans rests with the management of R&D, but a number of broad, execution-related issues demand thoughtful consideration by the CEO and the full management team. These issues involve (1) the organization of R&D across the corporation (centrally? by division? by business unit? geographically?), (2) the systems needed to relate the R&D organizations for effective communication and mutual reinforcement, and (3) the optimum reward systems for R&D professionals.

As in R&D portfolio planning, there is no clear-cut right or wrong approach to dealing with these issues, only a system of trade-offs to consider. Third generation R&D management distinguishes itself from earlier generations by consciously identifying these issues and making the trade-offs explicit.

Senior management is regularly faced with organizational questions. Figure 7-1 lists some typical questions and the underlying strategic issues they get at.

The way R&D is organized has a substantial impact on its effectiveness and efficiency. Inappropriate organizational structure can hamper the deployment of R&D talent, increase the cost of output, and delay results. It can increase the risk of unwelcome surprises due to external developments. Most damaging, suboptimal organization can lead to poor communication, poisoning the lifeblood of every R&D organization with barriers created both within the R&D organization and between R&D and the rest of the company.

If tactics are the use of forces to win an engagement and strategy is the use of engagements to win the objectives of a war, organization

Figure 7-1

Typical organization issues in R&D

TYPICAL ORGANIZATION QUESTIONS

Should we centralize or decentralize control of application development?

Should we integrate the R&D ability of our recent acquisition or manage it at arm's-length?

What changes in organization might reduce product-development lead-time?

Should we establish a market research capability within R&D?

Where, geographically, should we locate our R&D capabilities?

UNDERLYING STRATEGIC ISSUES

Is R&D responding adequately to business needs?

Is R&D responding to corporate goals?

Is R&D communicating effectively, internally and externally?

Is R&D attracting top scientists and engineers?

Is R&D using resources efficiently?

is the catalyst that facilitates the implementation of both tactics and strategy. Like a catalyst, the optimum organization is one that fits the combination of input conditions and the desired end state. When the organization is optimal and the targets are well chosen, a company can expect its R&D to be efficient and effective. In contrast, the cost of a suboptimum R&D organization can be enormous. In companies we have worked with to get the most out of R&D, we have uncovered wasted efforts and wasted opportunities easily worth 20 to 50 percent of total R&D expenditures.

Toward the Optimum Structure

There is rarely a clear-cut "best" way to structure R&D. The structure must balance partially conflicting interests and objectives. It must maximize responsiveness, provide a critical mass of human and capital resources, allow appropriate control, safeguard flexibility, and support both ongoing and new businesses.

Other driving forces for change in R&D establishments include (1) the rapid growth of the technologies that a typical company must master; (2) expansion of the R&D capabilities of the corporation; (3) an increasing need to support businesses on a global scale; (4) larger customer demands for responsiveness from the R&D establishment; and (5) the new degrees of organizational freedom offered by the rapid development of new information technologies. In addition, some organizational conditions are almost forced on R&D by changes in the conditions in which the business operates.

A good example of a company responding to change is Boehringer Ingelheim. With sales of DM 3.5 billion (about $2.1 billion in 1990 dollars) Boehringer Ingelheim is a medium-sized pharmaceutical company. In the 1960s, the company became the first German pharmaceutical house to set up subsidiaries in the United States and Japan. The U.S. subsidiary began research in the mid-1970s, the Japanese subsidiary in the early 1980s.

R&D decision making was almost completely decentralized: the research heads of each subsidiary could develop products specifically for their geographic markets. This was an appropriate structure for an aggressive, growing European company seeking market share in the United States and Japan, encouraging Boehringer Ingelheim to develop specific products for specific markets. But by the mid-to-late 1980s, as the pharmaceutical market became more competitive on a global basis, it became clear that top management was spending too much money on products that were not transferable from one market to another.

Today, Boehringer Ingelheim still maintains research centers in the United States, Italy, and Japan, as well as in Germany. However, strategic decisions about which products to develop for which markets by which research center are now made centrally, with input from an International Steering Committee made up of the heads of research, the heads of the medical departments, and the heads of marketing from all the major geographic subsidiaries and R&D centers.

Five Dimensions
of Structural Choice

Five structural elements of an R&D organization must be evaluated explicitly and simultaneously:

1. The use of internal versus external R&D resources
2. Centralized versus decentralized control and funding of R&D
3. Concentrated versus distributed R&D resources
4. An input orientation versus an output orientation
5. The balance between line and project management

Internal Versus External
R&D Resources

Management must decide whether to expend internal R&D resources to develop certain expertise, technologies, or products, or whether to go outside for them. Figure 7-2 illustrates some current moves outside.

Figure 7-2

Examples of "outside" or joint R&D

IBM and AT&T jointly sponsor superconductivity research

DSM and Toyobo join forces to develop the Dyneema superstrong polyethylene fiber

Siemens and IBM team up to develop 64-MB DRAMS

Philips, RCA, and Thomson cooperate in the development of high-definition television

Japanese companies pay for more than one-third of the corporately funded chairs at MIT

Industry-funded research at MIT doubles in the 1980s

The EC has committed over $20 billion to support international R&D consortia

In many companies the use of external R&D resources is considered as a last resort; and when it is done, it is undertaken on an ad hoc basis. But in third generation R&D management, working with external parties—whether in academia, government, or industry—is not only considered a viable option but is actively encouraged.

A number of technological and market forces drive companies toward external linkages. Among these are a proliferation of the technological content of products and services; the requirement to shorten development and lead-times; increasing interest and mutual understanding between business, government, and academic institutions; and simply a growing experience with joint R&D work.

Whether to use external R&D resources represents a classic make-or-buy decision, this time with reference to technology or R&D results.

With regard to the simple, binary make-or-buy decision, a company must take into account a number of variables, such as cost, time, and critical mass of resources. Third generation management tends to do the following:

- Buy base technologies when the organization doesn't already have the capability. By definition, base technologies are widely available, and the organization does not want to waste resources reinventing the wheel.
- Closely monitor pacing and emerging technologies using a variety of approaches: investing in universities, collaborating with companies in noncompetitive industries, participating in research consortia, and cooperating with government.
- Ensure control over R&D investments in key technologies because they embody the essence of protectable technological differentiation.

University-industry cooperation. The results have been decidedly mixed, but there has been significant progress in recent years. Today, certain market and financial forces are conspiring to push universities and industries closer together:

- The increasing pressure on the universities' internal funds and the lowering of government R&D funds, which make it necessary for universities to seek funding from industry
- The improved ability of both parties to negotiate practical contracts

- Increased entrepreneurship among academics
- Companies' better understanding that links with universities provide early access to large bodies of critically important, advanced knowledge and judgment

Industry is attracted to the quality of knowledge and brain power at universities but has often found it difficult to bridge the culture gap. Industry does not mistrust the university as much as it fails to understand it. Companies can be frustrated at what they perceive to be the unfocused objectives of academic science and the pace of academic research.

The university may fear the contamination of its pure, intellectual pursuits and the prostitution of science for profit. It may mistrust business people who, it feels, want to buy the potentially valuable output of its laboratories at modest prices. And the idea of proprietary knowledge may be in conflict with the notion of academic freedom and open exchange of ideas.

Despite these problems, many collaborations have succeeded.

Japanese companies are increasingly embracing American academic sources of technology. More than one-third of the 55 corporate funded chairs at the Massachusetts Institute of Technology are funded by Japanese companies at a price of over $20 million per year.

Collaborations contributed significantly to the development of DSM's Stanyl Nylon 4,6 engineering plastic. And in Britain, it is difficult to find a major university where ICI is not sponsoring work in chemistry and chemical engineering departments.

In the United States, major medical schools often have strong ties to pharmaceutical companies—Harvard and Massachusetts General Hospital with Hoechst; and Yale with Bristol-Myers Squibb, which recently built a major corporate research center a mere ten miles from the Yale campus.

Government-business collaboration. The idea of large-scale business-government collaboration has long been the purview of the Japanese. MITI and what Western business people often refer to as "Japan Inc." are legend. Today, the Japanese example in leading and coordinating industrywide and cross-industry collaboration is being followed in Europe, apparently with some success.

In Europe, the European Commission has committed over $20 billion to international R&D consortia and "precompetitive" cooperative projects. The Eureka program covers research in a broad range of key technologies. Esprit covers research in computers and communications technologies; Brite, in new materials and aeronautics technologies. Race seeks to develop technology for a Europewide high-speed data telecommunications network, and Comet sponsors work on exchanges, scholarships, and other university-business links.

In the United States, the focus of government-business links has been on help for small, entrepreneurial businesses rather than on increasing linkages with large companies. However, through the Defense Advanced Research Projects Administration (DARPA), the government since the 1960s has spent vast sums on fundamental scientific research at universities and has often continued this funding to small companies spun out of university labs by faculty members and venture capitalists. Rarely has America organized vast projects like those now being undertaken in Europe, although in the recent past, the country has moved to loosen some legal restrictions—most notably antitrust laws—and allow more business-business collaboration and linkage.

Business-business cooperation. In the increasingly important area of business-business cooperation, the United States expects rapid and considerable expansion as more companies begin to feel comfortable buying and sharing technology. The culture gaps to be bridged in this form of cooperation are often much smaller than in university-industry and government-business cooperation. Since companies are becoming increasingly aware that they cannot develop every missing piece of technological capability, they are finding innovative ways to merge expertise, such as the alliance of four European aerospace companies into the AIRBUS consortium.[1] Especially in the United States, however, the fear of government intervention still hinders but does not exclude this kind of activity, especially among large companies. Two examples are the IBM-Siemens alliance to make 64 megabit dynamic random access memory chips (DRAMS) after the collapse of U.S. Memories, Inc., a consortium of American companies that had hoped to develop these chips for the U.S. market,[2] and the alliance of RCA with Philips and Thomson to work on high-definition television (HDTV), an effort by a U.S. company to create both a short-term strategy of cooperation with a foreign-owned company to develop and manufacture HDTV and a longer-term strategy of building indigenous strength in underlying technologies such as displays, consumer chips, and electronics manufacturing.[3] Another example is the Motorola-Toshiba alliance, in which Motorola exchanged semiconductor technology for help in gaining market share in Japan.[4]

To accommodate the increasing recognition of the potential benefit of working with external parties, companies are beginning to make some important organizational changes, notably:

- Reinforcing their capability to manage outside contracts over a long period of cooperation rather than on a project-by-project basis
- Creating a corporatewide framework for make-or-buy decisions involving strategic technology
- Reinforcing the technology purchasing and selling functions and placing them at senior levels in the corporation

Many companies are creating "technology manager" positions at the divisional or corporate level. The technology manager monitors external technology developments for opportunities—as well as threats—and proposes initiatives as needed, helps divisional management determine technological priorities, fosters partnership relations and communications between R&D and the rest of the company, and develops global patenting and licensing strategies.

Centralized Versus Decentralized Funding and Control; Concentrated Versus Distributed Resources

These two elements are often seen as one and often dominate discussions about the organization of R&D. The pendulum frequently swings from centralized R&D to decentralization (distributed) and back again. In fact, there are two separate considerations, and treating them separately can often lead to the optimum organizational relationships.

The need to make R&D resources responsive to individual businesses and to rapid change in competitive conditions stimulates the decentralization/distribution of R&D resources (see Figure 7-3). However, companies often discover that this process can do serious damage by breaking up the critical mass of technological centers of excellence, by focusing resources on the near term, and by diminishing the quality of communication and cooperation between R&D centers.

Figure 7-3

*Potential strengths and weaknesses of decentralization
and distribution of resources*

ORGANIZATION APPROACH	STRENGTHS	WEAKNESSES
Decentralized control and funding	• Responsiveness • Accountability	• Short-term bias • Suboptimal use of scarce resources • Profitability threat to program continuity • Corporatewide interests fall between the cracks
Distributed R&D resources	• Responsiveness • Accountability	• Experience and cost penalty by breaking up critical mass • Loss of information • Reduced cross-fertilization • Decreased flexibility

But that need not happen. Communication and information technology offers new degrees of organizational freedom; it is no longer necessary to be physically close in order to communicate, cooperate, and maintain control. At the same time, increasing globalization is stimulating the distribution of R&D resources. Companies are responding to the separability of control and proximity in effective ways. The Boehringer Ingelheim example illustrated how well-centralized decision making can coexist with market and geographically distributed activities.

Third generation companies realize that what really matters for R&D performance is less who controls and funds than the quality of the communication and planning as reflected in the quality of the portfolio of projects that R&D undertakes.

Today, companies use a wide range of different R&D structures, often depending on the size of the organization. As Figure 7-4 shows, most large companies have at least one concentrated (central or corporate) R&D center working for multiple divisions and businesses and focusing on longer-term, higher-risk radical R&D projects and on building know-how. In addition, most have divisional or business unit laboratories concentrating on incremental R&D.

But within one industry, companies of comparable size use different R&D structures. Looking at the chemical industry, for example, in Figure 7-5, we see a broad range of approaches.

A few useful guidelines exist with regard to this dimension.

Figure 7-4

Companies with some centralized R&D resources as a function of company size

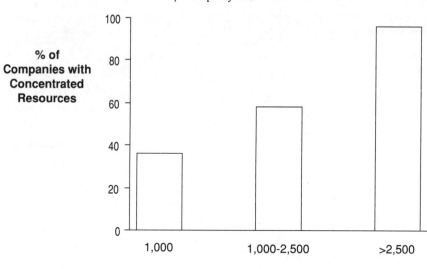

Source: EIRMA—based on a sample of European companies.

Fundamental and radical R&D benefits most often from concentrated (central) effort and from control and "protection" from immediate business pressures. Incremental work tends to benefit from R&D distributed to the divisions or businesses.

A second element to take into consideration is the degree to which an area of technological expertise is important to one division (or business) or to several across the corporation. When a technology is relevant to a single division, distribution/decentralization is an attractive option. When several divisions share the need for excellence in one or more technologies, centralized coordination and concentrated resources for research in these technologies may be the correct choice.

The need for companies to struggle with complex organizational issues in the R&D function continues to grow. In almost every situation today, forces are pushing for greater global efficiency, favoring concentrated resources and top-down, centralized decision making. These forces often include the costs associated with maintaining separate R&D facilities.

Figure 7-5

Control and resource configuration of R&D
in selected major chemical companies

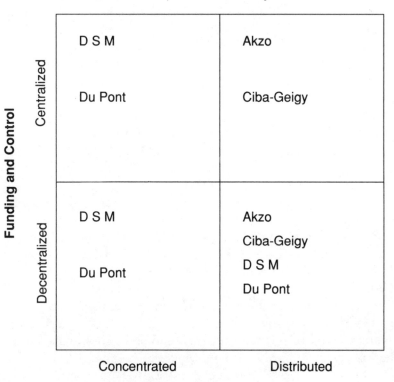

Resource Configuration

Pulling in the opposite direction are forces for local responsiveness, such as national regulatory bodies, local regulations, geographic product preferences, and local labor conditions. In the pharmaceutical industry, for example, regulations in specific countries often favor clinical testing that has been carried out in the local country during the product-approval process, prompting companies to decentralize portions of the drug-development process. Similarly, in some countries, higher (government-determined) prices are available for products if the pharmaceutical research is carried out locally, an example of regulations driving the dispersion of R&D. These forces all affected the thinking of Boehringer Ingelheim when it decided to maintain dispersed R&D activities despite centralizing decision making.

The desire to be close to the customer is a common factor that companies consider when choosing to disperse R&D activities geographically. Closeness to customers may include the requirement for local suppliers—especially those involved in consumer-product research to be close to individual markets to respond to local consumer preferences effectively. For example, many suppliers to the automotive industry are establishing R&D and production capabilities near their Japanese customers' decision-making centers to adapt, qualify, and supply products in Japan and to integrate closely with their customers' production capabilities.

Siemens has recognized that in order to make inroads in the U.S. medical instrumentation market, a strong American R&D presence is indispensable. Japanese companies in many industries came to a similar conclusion regarding the United States, where they have established over 100 R&D centers.

Access to key resources is a driving force behind some geographic dispersion of R&D. A number of companies are setting up R&D labs in Japan to attract Japanese research talent and to be near centers of Japanese technological excellence. Japanese and European companies place R&D centers in the United States for similar reasons.

Whatever the forces facing a specific industry, three tasks fall within the purview of third generation R&D management: harnessing the global proliferation of technology effectively, developing products suited to regional markets, and still exploiting the economies of worldwide product lines whenever possible.

In the past, companies have gravitated toward the structural solution that meets the majority of its needs—a concentrated structure if internal efficiency was the primary goal, a distributed structure if local needs for market proximity or response to external constraints were the primary drivers. Or, in more complex situations, a combination of concentrated and dispersed structures based on the type of R&D being conducted.

The way management works in a dispersed R&D situation varies. At Boehringer Ingelheim, despite the centralization of decision making, there has been a clear effort to keep the dispersed centers involved in setting priorities for the R&D portfolio. The International Steering Committee meets six times a year to work on the specifics of the portfolio, which projects will be undertaken, where the work will be done, what their funding level will be, and so forth. Another companywide body, the Forum, made up of senior research and business managers, works to make sure that the R&D strategy matches the overall company strategy. Line responsibility for non-German R&D units rests with the management of the local subsidiaries, which have considerable discretion within the overall guidelines of the R&D strategic plan to exploit local new-business development opportunities.

In a similar way, Becton Dickinson recently formed worldwide strategy teams around each of its major product groups to maintain central control over R&D execution—an important element in the company's strategy of global manufacturing-cost leadership—while obtaining the important participation of local managers in the decision-making process.

The Boehringer Ingelheim and Becton Dickinson examples of dispersed physical execution of R&D coupled with concentrated decision making provide the integrated network for R&D management. In this approach, companies focus on achieving high subsidiary involvement in R&D strategy formulation and implementation, very good management systems, and a strong sense of joint purpose and common goals throughout the organization.

Strong central guidance to dispersed R&D centers alone, without local participation and buy-in, is not a solution because local entrepreneurship and R&D drive are inventive in boycotting or bypassing the central control in which they have not participated and in which they feel no ownership.

Input-Oriented Versus Output-Oriented Structure

Another important issue affecting R&D resources is whether the organizational structure should be input oriented or output oriented. The decision is linked to the ability of the R&D establishment to fulfill two conflicting goals:

1. The activities of the various disciplines and specialties must be coordinated in order to accomplish the work of multidisciplinary projects. This coordination is best accomplished by output-oriented organizations in which units are organized by product or customer groups.
2. Projects must be provided with state-of-the-art information—through face-to-face communication—in the technolo-

gies they draw upon. The provision of such information is best accomplished by input-oriented organizations in which units are organized by scientific or engineering specialties and disciplines.

Figure 7-6 shows simplified models for input- and output-oriented R&D organizations.

The principal input to an R&D organization is technical and scientific knowledge. To handle this input effectively, R&D organizations have for years structured themselves around scientific disciplines, technologies, or technical specialties. This structure binds scientists and engineers comfortably to their technical specialties. R&D professionals maintain their technical competence partly through interactions with respected colleagues. The functional—or input-oriented—structure enables them to do this effectively by placing them in organizational and, often, physical proximity to colleagues who share their technical specialty.

Of course, by focusing so strongly on the input side of the equation, that form of organization can create difficulties on the output side, because the output of an R&D project is normally shaped not by specific technical disciplines or specialties but by an assembly of the many technical skills required to translate a primary R&D result into commercial success. Output takes its form in designs for new products or processes that require the simultaneous application and coordination of an appropriate blend of technical specialties. Organization by technical discipline or specialty creates difficult-to-manage barriers to coordination and arriving at the end result.

In the output-oriented organization, scientists and engineers are removed from their functional departments and are organized by the structure of the client base they seek to satisfy—that is, customer/product group. The simplest form of output-oriented organization is, of course, a single project. Most output-oriented organizations are multiproject. The output organization solves the coordination problem by ensuring that everyone shares the same reporting relationship, by providing the project manager with direct authority, and by bringing all the technical skills together in one organization with one purpose—achieving the objective of the project.

The project organization is effective for output but not, of course, without ancillary problems. Scientific and engineering knowledge is not organized in the form of projects and clients. Scientists and engineers immersed in a project structure are at risk to stay current with developments in their specialties. Over a long enough time—say,

Figure 7-6

Typical input- and output-based R&D structures (simplified)

**Line/Input
Organization**

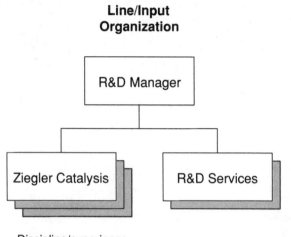

Discipline/experience-
based units

**Output/Product
Organization**

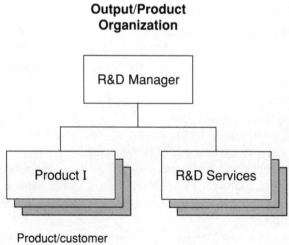

Product/customer
group-based units

Figure 7-7

Prioritizing technology sharing and synergy opportunities

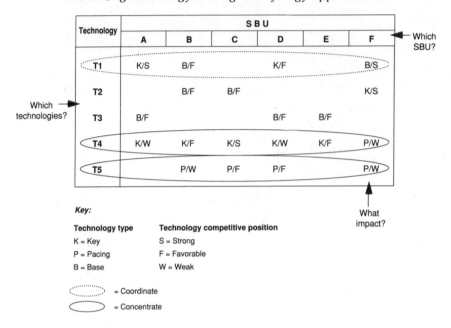

three years—members of the project team risk isolation from advances in their technical fields.

First generation management characteristically did not concern itself with the conflict between organization by technical discipline and organization by project. Structure by functional specialties was the only way to organize scientists and engineers.

Second generation management, applying more of the project concept, began using one-time project (output-oriented) teams. At the conclusion of the project, scientists and engineers were usually returned to their place in the functional structure. Typically, management power remained with the functional department head, rarely with the project manager. The potential for confusion in the minds of scientists and engineers about company loyalty and their future careers is apparent.

Third generation management consciously recognizes the conflict between functional and multidimensional work groups, loyalties, and career aspirations and purposefully seeks to balance the benefits and disadvantages of each for the long-term good of the individual researcher and the R&D organization as a whole. (See Figure 7-7.)

Several criteria influence the input/output orientation trade-offs that companies make when they decide on both their formal and their operational R&D organization structures. They look at the rate of change in the technical disciplines to which their researchers are attached. If the rate of change in technical disciplines is greater than is the rate at which the project can be completed, they tend to prefer the skill-based functional organization, the better for scientists and engineers to sustain their technical currency. If the rate of change is faster in the project than in technical disciplines, the preferred structure tends to be the output-based project system, the better to propel the project to completion. Clearly, management concerns with structure and staffing differ meaningfully between an R&D task that will be concluded in two years and one that will require five or six years.

As the rate of change in a particular technology slows, it may become appropriate to shift the structure from skill based to output oriented. For example, when biotechnology was new and new discoveries were revealed monthly, the biotechnology function was typically isolated as a separate department or even a separate company. Now, much (but certainly not all) of biotechnology is considered a "wrench of the bench." Its staff and competence may be spread widely within the company whose goals are to apply biotechnology in pharmaceuticals, animal care, agricultural chemicals, and diagnostic systems.

Line Versus Matrix Versus Project Organization

The final important question is whether to have a line or a matrix structure for the day-to-day management of an R&D enterprise and how the issue of "project management" fits in. Figure 7-8 offers three options. In a pure line—or functional—form, projects are assigned to a functional manager to coordinate. In a pure project form, each project is a self-contained unit including most, if not all, of the skills that are needed to execute the project, and key project functions are headed by a line manager. The matrix form couples features of both the project and the functional forms, with complementary lines of control and influence from the functional and project organizations.

Companies that undertake multiple projects simultaneously typically use some form of the matrix, whether they realize it or not. For instance, when members of a functional organization are put into

Figure 7-8

*The matrix organization is halfway between the input-
and output-oriented organizations*

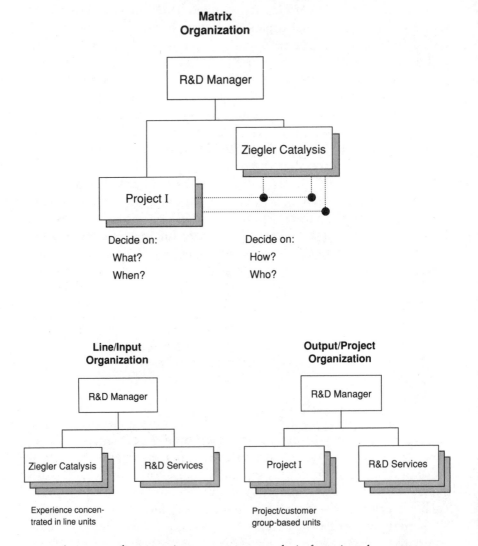

a project team but continue to report to their functional managers, a
form of matrix exists. How well any matrix type of organization
works depends on the balance of influence and control held by the
project manager and the line manager and on the clarity with which
individual researchers are assigned their responsibilities and loyalties.

The three structures have different sets of advantages, as shown
in Figure 7-9.

Figure 7-9

Advantages of different types of R&D organizations

	Line/Input Organization	Matrix Organization	Output/Project Organization
Resource efficiency	Medium	High	Medium
Resource flexibility	Medium	High	Low
Essential information flow	Medium	High	Medium
Clarity of relationships	High	Low	Medium
R&D/business integration	Weak	Moderate	Strong
Customer focus	Weak	Moderate	Strong

The maturity of the critical R&D technologies embodied in a project, their rates of change, and the pace of R&D of its task toward completion (perhaps the rate of market change) are useful guides in the selection of the appropriate combination of matrix and input or output organizational structure, depicted symbolically in Figure 7-10. The next chapter focuses more closely on project management and the challenge of managing the matrix.

Figure 7-10

Selecting appropriate combinations of "matrix plus"

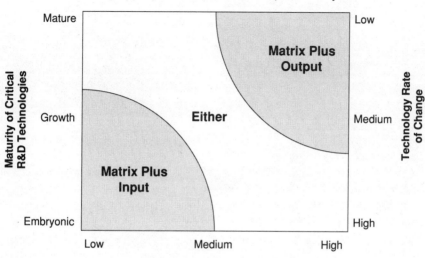

In discussing the options for organizational structure—none perfect—we have attempted to show that, because the conditions under which companies compete grow increasingly complex, the trade-offs that must be managed in developing an effective organizational structure for R&D also grow increasingly complex. The trade-offs cannot be managed sequentially; they must be dealt with simultaneously, as in a five-dimensional chess game. Relatively few normative guidelines exist to facilitate the complex process of reaching the correct balance for a specific company in a specific competitive environment. There is no perfect prescription for success, no right answer. But there is a right course of action for management. It is to recognize and explicitly act on the complexities and trade-offs for the benefit of the R&D objectives, the long-term good of individual researchers, and R&D as a vital, creative, and productive organization.

Notes

1. R. Lygo, "Strength in Numbers," *Management Today* (November 1989), p. 5.
2. Kim Clark, "What Strategy Can Do for Technology," *Harvard Business Review* (November–December 1989), p. 94.
3. Jeffery A. Hart and Laura Tyson, "Responding to the Challenge of HDTV," *California Management Review,* vol. 31 (Summer 1989), p. 132.
4. Bernard Avishai and William Taylor, "Customers Drive a Technology-Driven Company: An Interview with George Fisher," *Harvard Business Review* (November–December 1989), p. 107.

Chapter 8

Beyond Project Management

The best laid plans of mice and men . . .

Robert Burns

Research and development, by its nature, is filled with unknowns. Successful implementation of R&D and technology plans is fundamentally a process of reducing the uncertainty surrounding the outcome. As discussed in Chapter 5, research and development is always a process of discovery and invention, although the degree to which new findings are required varies by stage of development and by the characteristics of the technologies employed.

Without systems that ensure that original plans are monitored, modified, and made to happen in an optimum way, a number of symptoms can begin to appear within the R&D organization. Even if your company does the best possible job of planning—choosing the right things—pitfalls will turn up and midcourse corrections will inevitably be necessary. To do the right things right, senior management must put in place procedures that

1. Aid in ensuring the optimum execution of the individual project—a well-planned, realistic course of development
2. Allow continual reevaluation, not only of the progress of individual projects, but of their relative priorities and resource requirements

Without these systems the company may find that strategically correct projects are slowly transformed into misfits and mishaps.

Misfits

Misfits are R&D projects that, once completed, turn out not to fit with business and corporate strategies after all. Misfits most com-

143

monly occur in R&D-driven companies when objectives have not been consistently evaluated in a business framework. The misfit may be a consequence of imprecisely or ambiguously developed descriptions of (specifications for) the R&D objective at its initiation, midcourse discoveries that led R&D to alter the objective without the advice and consent of its business client, or midcourse changes in the business direction without an accompanying review of the supporting R&D programs.

Mishaps, in contrast, are R&D projects that do fit business strategies but are completed too late (or not at all) because one or more other functions in the organization is unprepared to fulfill its role in achieving the successful R&D result. Both misfits and mishaps are the result of poor planning, poor communication, and inadequate management coordination within the company.

Portents of trouble in R&D projects include several all-too-familiar symptoms.

Dithering

All projects have promise; most have drawbacks. Ditherers are projects that are evaluated and reevaluated, started, stopped, and restarted. When active, they are characterized by frequent changes in the course or pace of development. Although all projects should be periodically reconsidered, dithering is a sign of serious systems failures, the lack of effective project evaluation and prioritization, and perhaps an inability to make the difficult decision to terminate projects.

Chronic Crisis

Projects often need to move up in priority for any number of reasons—for example, a competitor's pending introduction of a similar product, newly discovered shortcomings in a product already on the market, or significant manufacturing problems. Reprioritization sometimes makes elementary good sense; but if undertaken repeatedly and routinely with a number of projects, it generates an atmosphere of chronic crisis. The crisis mode of resource reallocation deprives other projects of the resources necessary to complete their development in a timely fashion and thus reinforces and perpetuates the crisis atmosphere.

Relegation to the Eternal Back Burner

Projects placed on the back burner languish and are denied their fair turn at consideration for resources. Patent life and commercial opportunity slip away almost unnoticed. Management that relegates projects to the back burner is avoiding its responsibility to assess project value in a full strategic context.

Lost Projects

Some projects proceed normally through the development sequence until their results land on a desk from which there is no advance. If project tracking is poor, such projects may stagnate for months or die.

Returns to the Drawing Board

Projects in which the results must be modified significantly (reengineered) to fit manufacturing needs represent a fundamental failure of the project-planning system and the lack of jointly developed, realistic plans that integrate across functions in the corporation. Variations on this theme include projects that don't meet customer needs, manufacturing capabilities, or cost constraints and projects that lack data to substantiate claims for regulatory approval.

Edsel Projects

Ill conceived from the beginning, Edsel projects are usually born when power centers push hard behind the scenes for approval of a project that will be plainly unattractive in open review. Such projects unfairly commandeer resources in response to power rather than to thoughtful strategic consideration.

Overzealous Bootleggers

No company wants to stifle innovation through micromanagement. Most companies encourage or at least accept unauthorized flights of technical fancy, commonly called "bootleg" work, from respected researchers. Bootleg research has provided the seed for many substantial advances. But if R&D management allows bootleg work to consume resources allocated to the portfolios of authorized work, bootlegging will become a serious problem. Somehow, management must ensure the progress of major official projects while encouraging the independent creativity of its best researchers. In any event, the best, most motivated researchers are likely to find ways to carry their load in assigned projects while quietly testing their bootleg ideas.

Nothing-Better-to-Do Projects

Researchers sometimes admit that they work a project long after its lack of attractiveness becomes clear because no better ideas are available to pursue. The planning process may have narrowed the pipeline too early and may be failing to maintain a backlog of strategically correct ideas for activation when resources become available. Nothing-better-to-do projects represent a management planning and systems failure; they inevitably result in waste, dispirited researchers, and missed or delayed opportunities.

The challenges of managing R&D to avoid those problems include effective planning and successful communication across diverse organizational and functional boundaries with people of different backgrounds, training, and understanding. No one will argue that meeting these challenges is easy. Many books have been written on effective project management. We yield to them, emphasizing instead that third generation management goes beyond project management to the effective management of the entire R&D-business complex—over many projects in many different R&D settings and across the businesses, operating divisions, and the corporation as a whole. Third generation R&D managers must constantly seek to link all relevant parts of and persons in the organization, by means of a daunting but unavoidable process of continuous communication, interaction, cooperation, and, inevitably, compromise.

What to Achieve: Objectives

The ultimate objective of managing the R&D process for results is to increase the value to the company of its businesses and to create new businesses. R&D's role in value enhancement is usually expressed in one or more of these classic dimensions:

Cost: Control the costs of developing products and processes and lower the cost of manufacture.

Speed: Shorten product- and process-development cycles.

Quality: Ensure superior or at least competitive product quality.

Image: Maintain a reputation for high quality, innovativeness, responsiveness, and good corporate citizenship. Attend to R&D's ancillary responsibilities for environmental compliance, service, prosecuting an effective patent program, and the like.

Once the R&D plan is in place, closely integrated into business and corporate plans, how does third generation management operate to achieve these outcomes? Successful R&D organizations emphasize the following goals:

- Communications
- Linked structural interfaces
- Creating a sense of importance and urgency in individual researchers
- Transparency: sharing uncertainty
- Creating an atmosphere of freedom from fear of intelligent failure
- Willingness to kill projects
- Corporatewide optimization of resources

Communications

Earlier in this volume we dealt extensively with common failures in communications between R&D and senior management, business management, and the key functions of marketing and manufacturing. We discussed the destructiveness of these failures—inadequate R&D business plans, mutual distrust, frustration, false starts, and strategically inadequate results. R&D's contribution will never reach its full potential in that atmosphere. Although the failures are rarely attributable solely to R&D, leadership to establish effective, mutually respectful communications and trust may have to come from R&D and levels like that of the chief technical officer. All plans and all operations in a company are dynamic, all subject to change, rapid or slow but continuous. Third generation management recognizes the essential place of effective communications among all elements of the organization and dedicates itself to cultivating the exchanges, the interactions, and the building of mutual confidence, all in an environment of change. Third generation management deals with the exchange of attractive and unattractive truths about projects; their changes in probability, time, and cost; and the inevitable shifting of positions within the portfolio.

Linked Structural Interfaces

The CEO of a large multinational chemical company commented recently that he was concerned that production and marketing were integrated much too late into the R&D process.

"R&D has to become an integral part of our company," he said. "Today, R&D still lives its own life—as if in a fortress."

The development of new products is perhaps the most complex process that most corporations undertake. Regardless of the business, new product development involves multiple transfers of knowledge (and trust) within the company and with external partners: research to development to engineering and manufacturing; to regulatory compliance in many industries; to marketing; and to sales. The linkage with senior management is pervasive. The challenge of managing R&D for results is to develop these interfacial linkages so that, in the ideal case, linkages and transfers are automatic, hardly observed by their participants.

Creating a Sense of Importance and Urgency in Individual Researchers

In today's competitive environment, it is axiomatic that successful R&D requires a sense of urgency. The drive to reduce organizational boundaries, to increase the ease of manufacturability of products from the R&D pipeline, and to bring more parts of the organization to bear on R&D earlier stems from the competitive imperative to bring new products and processes to fruition faster.

In today's business environment, the time value of R&D results is significant in almost every industry. Obtaining a lead over competitors can translate into long-lasting market advantage, whether the lead is measured in weeks, as in the toy or garment industries, or in years, as in pharmaceuticals or automobiles. The value of acceleration is high; the ability to instill a strong sense of urgency becomes a crucial element of managing for results.

Analysis of the profit drives associated with an automobile R&D program demonstrated, for example, that reducing lead-time by 20 percent has a far greater impact on profitability than cutting R&D or capital investment by an equal or even larger amount. This benefit is based only on the difference in product introduction dates and does not include the upside potential of earlier introduction such as enhanced market share.

Management's role in creating a sense of urgency is multidimensional. Contrary to practices we have observed in industry, it has nothing to do with threats, exhortations, or the whipping syndrome. Rather, it has everything to do with conveying to research teams the importance of the R&D objective, the importance of time, and the vital role of each individual acting in concert with others to achieve the objective. In short, a climate of excitement is a far more powerful driver of accomplishment than is a climate of fear.

Transparency: Sharing Uncertainty

Openness and transparency of purpose and of progress—key characteristics of successful third generation management—represent a cultural willingness to use a common language, mutual reliance, and trust to work confidently toward the objectives of R&D projects, reduce uncertainty, and shorten lead-times.

The high costs of the absence of transparency lead to difficult R&D management problems, as units of the organization withhold information to protect key projects or people. R&D journals are ripe with examples (typically recalled fondly and proudly by researchers) of R&D projects that were hidden—bootlegged—from the transparency of broader scrutiny in the belief that business management would not understand, support, or share their attendant uncertainties. Many of R&D's great successes are marked with such tales. The story of Tagamet's development, for example, is one of an isolated group of researchers working on a forbidden project, hidden from corporate scrutiny by a protective R&D boss.[1] Of course, we hear of the occasional success, but not of the uncountable failures.

As interesting and satisfying to R&D as the stories of occasional success may be, the development of a culture in which such stories persist unchecked represents a fundamental failing perhaps of R&D management but more probably of general management. Although initiative research can be an important part of an R&D portfolio (as shown in Chapter 6), the uncontrolled proliferation of bootleg projects, with the diffusion of resources over goals of uncertain quality, is a far more common outcome in a culture that lacks transparency and the willingness to share risk.

Creating an Atmosphere of Freedom from Fear of Intelligent Failure

As important as increasing the organization's openness and transparency is the need to reduce the fear of failure. If R&D undertakes a bold but thoughtfully conceived initiative and makes clear the uncertainties associated with it, and if the work is intelligently and diligently prosecuted but nature's laws prevent arriving at the desired result, the project is a failure (although valuable knowledge might have been accumulated). A 1989 National Science Foundation study found that the fear of failure was cited most frequently by researchers as the primary barrier to innovation in their organizations.[2]

The way organizations define objectives and the consequences that result when objectives are not met offers key insights into the existence or lack of third generation management. For example, unreasonable penalties set for good technical work that, despite intelligence, creativity, and commitment, fails to yield the sought-after results are clearly at odds with third generation thinking and are certain to discourage technical initiative. If intelligent failure is punished, researchers will undertake only sure projects, which provide safety but scant competitive advantage.

Willingness to Kill Projects

When Thomas Edison was asked if he was discouraged by his lack of progress in finding a material that would work as a durable filament in the incandescent lamp, he replied, "No, because I've found 99 things that don't work."

Edison persisted with his project and eventually produced a commercially viable light bulb. Many projects, however, should end—respectively—at Edison's midpoint conclusion: the discovery of things that don't work.

A key but difficult responsibility of R&D management is the delicate one of deciding when to terminate a project even though project team members are optimistic about overcoming remaining barriers. In third generation management, there is a sensible way to terminate R&D projects while retaining the staff's interest, enthusiasm, and esteem. An effective termination decision demands sensitivity to the personalities of team members who have invested heavily in the project, as well as technical answers, business judgment, and communication skills that prompt the project team to respect the decision and move enthusiastically on to the next task.

Corporatewide Optimization of Resources

Finally, the spirit of managing for results in the third generation has as its objective the ongoing optimization of corporatewide resources. Killing, reinforcing, and adding projects should be undertaken without excessive concern for organizational boundaries. Optimizing the allocation of scarce resources for the corporation as a whole must always be in the management repertory in the third generation.

What to Do: Seven Key Practices

How can managers, both CEOs and R&D managers, assure themselves that their organizations are developing and institutionalizing practices consistent with third generation management? Much experience argues that seven key practices or characteristics will help manage the process effectively:

- The existence of a common vocabulary for describing and characterizing R&D projects and their objectives, allowing rigorous communication
- A process that jointly develops clearly articulated, mutually agreed-upon, strategically evaluated project objectives, with clearly defined results

- A process for setting priorities and allocating scarce resources—capable of change in response to market, strategic, technological, and competitive developments
- A backlog of ideas
- An aggressive approach to project design that addresses most significant technical uncertainties as early as possible—that is, a willingness to "stand 'em up and shoot"
- A practical approach to individual project planning, reporting, measurement, and control, aided by appropriate information systems
- An appropriate project-team structure, composition, and authority—the professional management of complex projects—along with appropriate integrative mechanisms

As shown in Figure 8-1, each practice plays an important role in helping an organization achieve the objectives discussed earlier in this chapter.

Figure 8-1

Managing for results

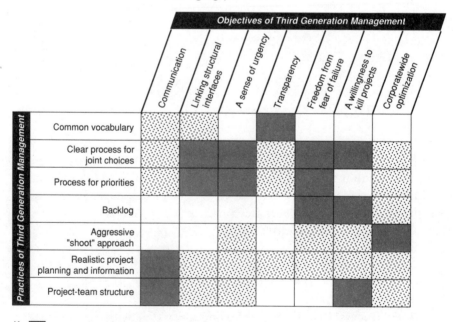

Common Vocabulary

The marketing vice president of the Haber Food Ingredients Division is frustrated. Months ago his competitors introduced a new salad dressing that, frankly, tastes great.

To compete successfully, he needs a new salad dressing that will taste better and cost less to manufacture. But his discussions with R&D seem to be going nowhere.

Once again, he reads a report from R&D. It describes in detail an intense effort to develop a new emulsifier system. The report talks about how close R&D is to achieving progress on an emulsifier system. Nowhere does it talk about salad dressing.

The frustration experienced by Haber's marketing vice president is not uncommon. Often R&D thinks of its goals—and describes them—simply in terms of demonstrating the feasibility of technological systems or approaches. Business, however, thinks in terms of products, markets, and financial goals. In the minds of the Haber R&D department, success with its emulsifier will significantly improve the taste of salad dressings and reduce manufacturing costs. But R&D's reports in no way connect the realities of the emulsifier project with the flavor and cost expectations of the marketing vice president.

Another way to think about the problem is that R&D often communicates data while the marketing vice president needs information in the way that Peter Drucker defined information, as "data endowed with relevance and purpose."[3]

A key component of successful communication in third generation companies is the ability to express R&D objectives and business objectives in a common language. That language needs to describe the technical means and relate them to the business ends in terms acceptable and clear to both technologists and business people.

Developing Clear Joint Objectives, Setting Priorities, and Allocating Resources

Movement from a sound strategy through successful implementation—by project, by multiproject business, by multibusiness division, and across the corporation—requires an iterative process for setting

Figure 8-2

Linking strategic planning to project planning and execution

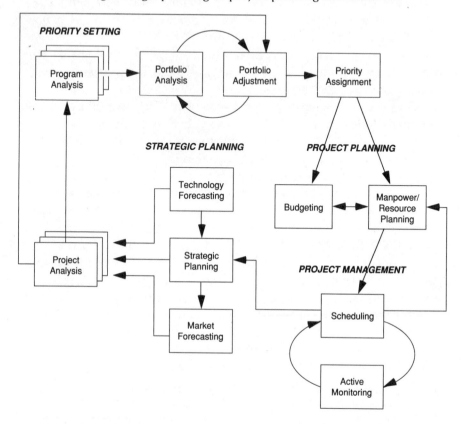

priorities and allocating resources in light of business and corporate objectives. Figure 8-2 shows the process used in one major medical products company.

Technical strategies are translated into specific programs that go through a portfolio review process similar to the one described in Chapter 6. The portfolio review sets priorities among the projects and allows subsequent resource planning, including detailed staffing requirements, to be developed. Systematic means to estimate resource needs are essential to effective priority setting, as represented symbolically in Figure 8-3.

The projected resource needs feed into a project management system that, as one of its outputs, provides status reports on the programs feeding back into the next year's technology planning and strategic planning cycle. Outlining the integrated process in this way

Figure 8-3

Assessing resource needs

Each project has projected resource needs

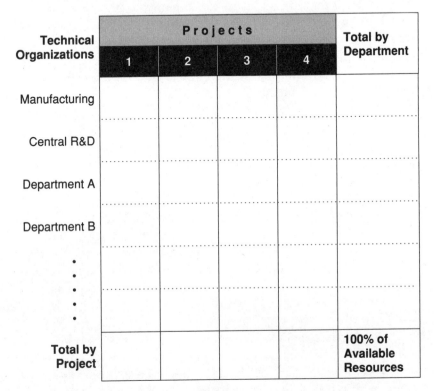

Technical Organizations	Projects				Total by Department
	1	2	3	4	
Manufacturing					
Central R&D					
Department A					
Department B					
⋮					
Total by Project					**100% of Available Resources**

allows everyone in the company to understand the process, the need for well-considered trade-offs within R&D objectives, the rationale for difficult decisions, and the fit of individuals and individual organizations within the whole. The process must not be seen to produce winners and losers. The corporation as a whole is the only winner, and the process encourages buy-in and support (or, at least, acceptance) by business and R&D participants.

A Backlog of Ideas

People are more inclined to say, "Enough is enough," and go on to the next project when the next project is clearly defined, clearly attractive, and only awaiting resources. A useful tool to encourage organizations to kill projects and avoid the lingering death that can drain corporate resources is to create a backlog of attractive pending projects.

One company has a policy of always having 25 percent more work defined than its resources can support. The company feels that such a policy maintains a healthy R&D balance. The backlog is used by management (1) as a test to ensure that the most attractive projects are supported and (2) to encourage among researchers receptivity to project termination in the knowledge that important alternative projects await them.

A Willingness to "Stand 'Em Up and Shoot"

One company faced a fascinating challenge. A new technology, developed somewhat accidentally in its R&D laboratory, had a wide range of potential applications, all of which were outside the current scope of the corporation. Over the course of its development efforts, the company asked for help in assessing the market potential and technological and competitive challenges facing the products that would result.

An early assessment described a large number of possible applications as well as the great uncertainty associated with any estimates of market size in view of the fact that none of the products had actually been tested. Several years later, little of significance had been added to the knowledge of market potential. The number of possible applications to which this fascinating technology could be applied was still vast; the potential revenues were still enormous; but uncertainty about any market estimates was significant.

What happened?

Over the years, the company had invested in significant technical development. It had dealt with a number of thorny issues surrounding the company's manufacturability and stability, and it had succeeded in producing a compound with extraordinary shelf life. But the technical work had failed to deal with the fundamental issues affecting the technology's commercial potential. In effect, the company had avoided subjecting the program to the toughest test—it had not pushed it up to the wall and pulled the trigger.

R&D and business management must be pushed to maximize the quality of the information developed through R&D investments, allowing decisions to be made as early as possible about key make-or-break issues in the product-development cycle. The sought-after results must be defined in such a way that if the critical demands fail to be satisfied, the fatal blow will be recognized as early and as inexpensively as possible.

Realistic Planning, Reporting, and Control, Accompanied by an Appropriate Information System

Managing for results in the third generation mode requires realistic projections of time, cost, and manpower needs. To ensure sound business results and to avoid compromising its future credibility, R&D's business partners must be equally demanding—and demanded of. They must provide the best quality information about markets, competitive dynamics, rates of environmental change, costs, and uncertainties surrounding market entry—the full commercial half of the success equation.

Controlling requires decision-oriented information for line, project, and top management.

Project plans are prepared jointly by the project manager, the department heads of the line organizations, and the internal customer. These plans include the commercial and scientific objectives of the project, its constituent individual activities, timing, costs, and, critically, milestones. These plans are the basis for comparison between actual and planned performance and for companywide, multi-project planning.

The tracking of performance against the project plan is often aided by visual displays of the project's flow. Pert and Gantt charts are frequently used tools, too well treated in other literature to be discussed in detail here. Though potentially useful, they tend to portray R&D as a disciplined, orderly, exactly forecastable process, which of course it is not. R&D is never precise. Good management incorporates in the project plan the assumptions for success that must be tested and the uncertainties that characterize creative work and then allows flexibility for timely plan revisions.

Project Team Structure, Composition, and Authority

As discussed in Chapter 7, many R&D projects are complex enough to justify a formal project-management system designed to cope flexibly with change, unanticipated challenges, and complex interorganizational interfaces. In those situations traditional, departmentalized thinking has to be changed to an interdisciplinary project orientation. Our work with clients, as well as a study done by R. Katz and T. J. Allen on 86 R&D teams in nine technology-based organizations,[4] shows clear improvements in tying R&D objectives to business strategy when R&D projects are undertaken in a multidisciplinary, output-oriented fashion.

We have alluded to the many good books about managing a single project. Third generation management, however, thinks about and practices project management as part of a holistic management system, as managing projects across business units, operating companies, divisions, and the corporation as a whole. Third generation project management could never be captured by a software package; it demands an understanding of and a sensitivity to the other key practices discussed in this chapter.

There is no assurance of success, but to encourage its probability third generation management considers project management and managing the interactions of multiple projects as a constructive overlay on the existing organizational structure, not as a competitor to it. The project manager and team provide crucial input to both the results to be expected and the resource-management processes: the technological objective, the work plan, resource requirements, and cost/benefit and risk/reward assessments. The project manager and team also require and obtain crucial information from the business system: the business purpose/objective and priority, market requirements, market potential and market uncertainty, state-of-the-art information on relevant external technologies, and resource availability over time. In obtaining and providing these inputs, the project manager and team deal with an increasing number of people both inside and outside the company.

In practice, the word *project* is commonly reserved for sizable clusters of activities with a clear beginning and a clear end; smaller activities or groups of activities are often referred to as *tasks* that do not need full project-management treatment. A "pure" project organization, with a task-force structure, is typically used in exceptional cases involving large resources. All project participants are transferred from their original department to the project team for the duration of the project. Administratively, functionally, and organizationally each member reports to the project management (a reporting structure that may lead to reorientation problems in functional departments at the end of a project). The great chemical company Hoechst, for example, makes these total transfers to a project when a new business unit is likely to evolve from the work.

For most projects, however, the matrix organization is optimal. People working on the project team stay hierarchically within their departments. In addition, the function of project manager is introduced. The project manager is disconnected from his or her original department and derives authority from well-established and visible linkages with senior R&D and business management.

During introduction of the matrix organization, clear rules of the game must be established between project and line managers. This can be done by means of a functional diagram that describes the tasks, responsibilities, and authorities of the project manager, each member of the team, and the line managers to whom the team members continue to report. The relationships must define the following:

- The objective of the team and the importance of the objective to the company.
- The responsibilities and authorities of the project leader, who is responsible for project coordination and overall results.
- The composition of the team, which is likely to change during the course of the work. Volunteers are more valuable and productive than conscripts.
- The responsibilities and role of the line managers to whom team members continue to report. The team member will want to know—should demand to know—who is responsible for his or her performance evaluation and career development.
- The milestones, cost and time parameters, and overall business expectations of the team.
- The reporting relationships of the team. Typically, team members will report to the team itself, to the senior R&D and business sponsors of the work, and to the line managers with whom team members continue an important relationship.

For all types of projects, a clearly defined client relationship is indispensable. The client's task is to define *what* and *when*, review progress and provide feedback, and fund the project. In diversified companies typical clients include divisional R&D coordinators/technology managers, corporate planners, and R&D itself. In companies that set up a steering committee, that committee itself often acts as the primary client.

At the outset, the "success" of a project must be defined in terms of the ideal profile of the product or process to be developed. Success will always have multiple parameters. They must be ranked by relative importance: those that are "killers"—meaning the project must be stopped if they cannot be achieved—must be clearly understood up front by all concerned.

The management decision that is most important for the success of a project is the choice of a project manager. The project manager is responsible for—and owns the authority for—all tasks that must be performed during a project and for the results vis-à-vis the client. The project manager plans, supervises, and leads the subtasks and end result, defines goals, and deals constantly with time and cost parameters.

Because the project manager plays the role of "entrepreneur" within the organization, he needs clear rights and authority in relation to the line organization. In badly established matrix project systems, the project manager is more a project administrator than a leader because he lacks sufficient authority to run the project in the face of interference from line management.

In order to be effective, the project manager must have a project budget that he controls. Experience in R&D organizations across all industries shows that a project manager is accepted by the line departments only if he has a budget with which to "buy" services from the line departments. Access to money confers access to control, stature, and respect.

A key element of systemwide project management is the founding of interdisciplinary teams and close, mutually supportive working relationships among them. Especially during the introduction of multidisciplinary project teams, problems may arise because technical specialists are not accustomed to dealing interdependently with other functional specialists or groups. Members of interdisciplinary teams must be rewarded for cooperation, for understanding the important roles of different disciplines, and for cooperation toward the achievement of the greater good. Led and supported properly—that is, in the mode of third generation management—effective teamwork is not difficult to achieve and it can be immensely rewarding to the individual, the project team, and the company.

This is not to suggest that there is a "cookbook" solution to project management—far from it. Establishing effective project management and coping with the interactive complexities of managing multiple projects simultaneously are among the most difficult of management assignments. Correctly executed in the correct strategic environment, they are among the management tasks most satisfying professionally and rewarding commercially.

Notes

1. P. Ranganath Nayak, and John D. Ketteringham, *Breakthroughs!* (New York: Rawson Associates, 1986).
2. "Barriers to Innovation in Industry—Opportunities for Public Policy Changes," National Science Foundation sponsored study by Arthur D. Little, Inc., and Industrial Research Institute (NSF C748 and C725).
3. Peter Drucker, "The Coming of the New Corporation," *Harvard Business Review* (January–February 1988), pp. 45–53.
4. R. Katz and T. J. Allen, "Project Performance and the Locus of Influence in the R&D Matrix," *Academy of Management Journal,* vol. 28, no. 1 (March 1985), pp. 67–87.

Chapter 9

Getting the Most Out of Your People: Breaking R&D Isolation

Interaction between research, business planning and marketing must be forced. It simply will not happen naturally.
Philip Smith, CEO, General Foods

Between the two a gulf of mutual incomprehension—sometimes hostility and dislike, but most of all a lack of understanding.
C. P. Snow, *The Two Cultures and the Scientific Revolution*

General managers are increasingly concerned with getting the most out of their R&D people, but many don't quite know how. They are anxious to keep R&D people motivated but have not found the magic formula to do it. Our clients constantly ask questions relating to motivation:

- Should rewards go to individuals or to teams?
- Should the reward be immediate or deferred?
- Should the reward be public recognition, money, or both?
- Should bonuses be part of the R&D compensation package?
- Should R&D personnel be given a share of royalties or earnings?
- How liberal should a company be about permitting technical publication by those on the staff to whom publication is important?
- Should recognition of superior performance be through promotion within the R&D hierarchy, or might other mechanisms—such as freedom to choose assignments—be more effective?

Although recognizing contributions and achievements is important, third generation management realizes that it cannot get the most out of R&D people by merely providing a multiplicity of motivating rewards. Rewards are cosmetic until the roots of motiva-

163

tion—R&D's emotional and often physical isolation and separation from corporate strategy—are dealt with. Although the human relations approaches that should be used in R&D differ little from those used in other areas of the corporation, it is important for managers to actively consider the "people element" of the R&D effort when seeking ways to get R&D to do the right things and do them in the right way.

One of the foremost tasks of third generation R&D management is to integrate the people of R&D into the larger corporate culture, to absorb R&D into full partnership with the businesses and the corporation. The isolation of R&D must be broken for at least these four reasons:

- To help avoid technology surprises—from within the company's R&D function or from sources external to the company—through a sharing of knowledge, experience, and intuition
- To encourage the people of R&D to identify with business goals and objectives and to make their work more purposeful and responsive by allowing them to participate in priority setting
- To enhance the status and contribution of the people of R&D by encouraging them to stimulate and to challenge business choices
- To improve the overall quality of management in the company through cross-fertilization between R&D and other company functions

Most of today's R&D and business managers and staff were brought up in environments and cultures that perpetuated isolation. The artificial walls between business and R&D are the result of the different cultural and educational backgrounds of R&D people and business people, the lack of a common language between them, technologically trained R&D managers' lack of familiarity with the practices of business management, and nontechnologically trained business managers' lack of familiarity with the workings of R&D and the mysteries of science and technology. Even technically trained business managers frequently do not have, or do not provide, the time for insight into R&D's efforts, particularly when the time frame for completion of the work is long.

The isolation is aggravated by the still common practice of locating R&D laboratories away from the company's other activities. It is further aggravated in some companies by the managerial autonomy of R&D, which functions like a mini-company within the company, operating within its own culture and "protected" from the rest of the organization.

Concerted and interrelated measures are needed to break this isolation. The first measure, we repeatedly stress, is the creation of a common language and system to link R&D, technology, and business strategy. Another is powerful strategic R&D planning. Both are discussed earlier in this book. In this chapter, we focus on three additional measures:

- Matching R&D resources with needs rather than matching work to resources
- Building on R&D personnel's people skills and traits, not just on their specialist characteristics and technical expertise
- Motivating R&D people through partnership, not just rewarding them for services rendered

Matching R&D Resources with Needs

In many companies, R&D departments are temples to specialization in particular scientific disciplines or fields of engineering. It all starts with hiring. The largest intake into the R&D department consists of bright young graduates hired to fill a vacancy in the laboratory for a particular specialist in next year's budget. When they arrive, they are assigned to the research group with which they have a disciplinary affiliation.

Hiring and organizing by discipline are perhaps necessary and certainly not at all bad, but they contribute to R&D isolation. The individual's scientific discipline or field of engineering becomes the major factor in the assessment of his performance—against that of peers in the same discipline—and in assignment to a particular project. The narrower the field and deeper the expertise, the greater is the danger of isolation.

A young hireling who succeeds stays in research. Unsuccessful hirelings may be "banished" to development or perhaps to production. Those who know how to maneuver politically may stay in research and become managers. Obviously, some talented researchers move into other functions, perhaps marketing, or become managers of R&D, but more often than not a talented researcher who wishes to stay on the bench is allowed to do so.

Mobility out of research and development is typically one-way mobility. The direction of this flow not only engenders isolation but also establishes an informal and unhealthy hierarchy among the technological functions: research is first in the pecking order, followed by development, then production, then engineering, and finally technical services. Yet none of these functions is sufficient unto itself in industrial R&D, and none should rank higher than the others.

Although the mobility of R&D people is typically one-way, the traditional mobility of business managers—designed to prepare them for general management by rotating them through a variety of functions—stops at R&D's door. Only R&D people are deemed competent to manage research and development. R&D promotes from within the function even when the company recruits from outside. It is rare to find an R&D manager whose educational background is nontechnical or whose prior work experience does not include R&D (notwithstanding that chief technology officers, whose responsibilities span a number of technology functions including R&D, often come from engineering or production).

For confidentiality, if for no better reason, R&D prefers to work within the R&D organization, rather than "buying" technological results. R&D management is inclined to maintain the capacity to do all work inside. Few managers willingly reduce staff in order to "buy" external resources. Doing so, after all, might diminish their stature.

Working in-house is fine if R&D practices active resource planning and always has more worthy projects waiting in line than it can support. But if this is not the case, there is the prospect of undertaking R&D work decided by the resources available rather than work that is strategically correct.

To match R&D resources to needs, third generation companies integrate recruiting, training, and career development into their R&D strategy.

First, they plan their resources over a five- to ten-year horizon. R&D management seeks to ensure that internal resources are consonant with near-term and anticipated requirements, and it seeks to ensure that resources are always under pressure and never exceed need. R&D management adopts a policy of sourcing from the outside whenever possible in an attempt to keep internal resources small—not only to keep costs down but to maintain flexibility and avoid short-term overstaffing and the potential of demoralizing cutbacks. Furthermore, the recruiting net is cast wide in order to avoid the development of narrow mini-cultures.

Second, third generation companies balance expertise against other attributes in assessing individual performance. They take total individual attributes into account in hiring individuals and assigning them to tasks and, when project structures are in place, in seeking team balance and manageability. Above all, they pay attention to the traits and skills of the project leader and ensure that these mesh with those of the rest of the team, not just with project objectives. The managers of important projects are professionals at managing; they are given authority to mobilize resources and exercise control; they are accountable; and they enjoy equal status with line managers in R&D as joint and crucial contributors to success.

Third, third generation companies signal clearly throughout the organization that they attach great importance to technology and its contribution to current and future profitability. They frequently empower a board-level chief technology officer (CTO) to integrate technology/R&D strategies and plans and to support and control their implementation. But they do not stop at the top; a key responsibility of the CTO is to ensure that corporate technologies—those shared between business units—are managed to exploit synergy and that all technological functions down the line work together and complement each other well.

Another key responsibility of the CTO is to sensitize fellow board members as well as general managers and functional managers in the corporation at large to the dynamics of R&D, including—most importantly—the uncertainty attendant upon good R&D. Third generation companies redefine failure in R&D to exclude the simple failure to meet targeted results and to include the nonexertion of effort and the failure to take reasonable risk. By redefining the objectives of every project to include the purposeful reduction of uncertainty, they make failure in its classical sense respectable.

Fourth, third generation companies rotate into R&D, not just out of it. They refute the principle of the sanctity of R&D management.

One large U.S. company appointed as head of R&D the manager of one of its product divisions. The individual in question had never worked in R&D before, although he was an engineer by training.

A European packaging company took the radical step of appoint-

ing its manager of international marketing—an economist by training—to head R&D. The individual had already gained the respect
of R&D people by helping them understand and respond to their
global customers' requirements.

In taking such a proactive stance, third generation companies
assert their belief that management is predominantly the ability to
lead, motivate, and get the most out of people in any setting. By so
doing, they help demystify R&D.

They also refute the principle of the one-way mobility of R&D
staff. One company rotated a particularly competent engineer responsible for the design and development of electro- and opto-power
devices back from development to central research—from which he
had come—to lead the unit providing fundamental and radical R&D
support to development in the same fields.

In such cases, research is responsive to the needs of development.
The two speak a common language, and informal relations and
friendships are able to overcome formalistic obstacles.

Building on People Skills and Traits

In many companies, R&D people are viewed by others as intro-
verted and uncommunicative, more interested in scientific and technological novelty than in commercial utility. The creative ones
among them easily develop prima donna tendencies. In such environments and cultures, the people of R&D are not trusted to deal with
commercial realities or to take part in business decisions. The thinking is: "Leave them alone; let them do their thing; and hope they
produce results."

This attitude places the company's future technology and even its
very viability in the hands of the technologists. It can also discourage
the researchers themselves, often with tragic human consequences,
as seen in the following case of freedom without a business purpose.

A company's research team leader had been allowed to work for
five years on his brainchild for a novel manufacturing process. When
he completed the project, he was encouraged by his R&D manager
to prepare a proposal for a capital appropriation and was asked to
present the proposal to the board. When he appeared before that
august body, he discovered that it was hearing about his project for
the first time.

Irritated at the waste of their time, the board members asked him to compress his one-hour presentation to fifteen minutes and then dismissed the proposal out of hand as irrelevant and inconsequential. The team leader was shattered. His disillusionment caused him to turn to drink. Now, several years later, he can be seen walking the corridors of his company, delivering the office mail, evidently unable to hold any other job. An extreme outcome perhaps, but unfortunately not rare. In this sad event, who failed? The researcher? Probably not. His management? Probably. Who paid the price of failure? The researcher, certainly. The company, probably.

In companies that look upon R&D people as special, there is a dual tendency, first to emphasize technological expertise over human traits and second to stereotype the human traits of R&D people into two broad categories:

> *"R"-types, or scientists:* Synthetic, spatial, and intuitive in their thinking, endowed with highly developed right-brain capacities, capable of lateral thinking, creative, and innovative—at least in their early, most productive years—say, before age forty!
>
> *"D"-types, or engineers:* Mostly left brained, analytical, digital, and deductive in their mindsets, thus wedded to vertical thinking and best at reactive, adaptive tasks. They also age well!

Social scientists who research the personality traits most suited to research and development aid and abet this stereotyping by categorizing R&D people into efficient innovators, or all-around researchers; inefficient innovators, or all-out idea people; efficient adapters, best suited for development tasks under clear instructions; and inefficient adapters, or failed, misplaced researchers.

Moreover, in companies such as we have described, the people of R&D perceive themselves as special people, a sort of elite, blessed with above-average intelligence quotients, education quotients, and ego quotients. They pride themselves on basing their decisions on expertise rather than on opinion and on behaving professionally rather than expediently. They see themselves as the guardians of the seed corn of the business and of its long-term well-being, immune to pressures and blandishments to achieve short-term results.

Though broadly useful, these categorizations and stereotypes ignore the immensely different dynamics and requirements of the various activities undertaken under the banner of R&D. In fundamental R&D, for example, more than creativity is necessary for successful work. For every bright hypothetical idea, a great deal of systematically rigorous follow-through is required. Furthermore, even if a large number of R&D people doing development work are of the disciplined type, happy to be told what to do, surely innovative types contribute additional benefit.

Each type of R&D—indeed, each project—requires a particular mix of technical expertise as well as human traits and skills. Yet, traditionally, R&D management in the West has focused more on individual technical expertise in hiring and career development and less on the enhancement of individual traits and skills. The same bias is evident in assigning researchers to projects. Insufficient attention is paid to the complementarity of skills and traits required to undertake the tasks at hand—in striking contrast to the Japanese approach.

Despite the feeling and perception of specialness, R&D personnel in many companies suffer a sense of inferiority within the company. They represent a cost that is not always easy to justify. Their work is singularly characterized by uncertainty over long periods of time, and its results are hard to measure. The bolder the work they undertake, the more frequently it ends in failure. Furthermore, they are not included in the company's higher councils, in which strategy is hammered out—even when technology is crucial to success. Also, they know that they are generally paid less than their peers in marketing and finance.

Partly because of their sense of inferiority and partly because of their fear of failure, R&D people have built a protective wall of cynicism around themselves, a sort of fortress R&D.

Third generation managers are not content to accept as a given the special traits of R&D people. They seek to understand and build on R&D people's human traits and skills as a complement to their technical expertise. Third generation managers realize that right-brain and left-brain capacities can be developed, that recognition can influence behavior, that various tasks are best accomplished by the proper mix of traits and skills, and, above all, that stereotyping individuals can stifle motivation and stunt development.

Furthermore, third generation managers make use of the ability of the majority of individuals to learn new skills and change. They also recognize that the learning and changing can be sources of motivation and rejuvenation for their people.

Finally, third generation managers recognize that desirable traits and skills such as creativity and innovation do not necessarily peak and then degenerate with advancing age. However, they do recognize the degenerative effect of isolation and overspecialization and are therefore alert to the needs of R&D people to continually see the "light at the end of the tunnel." They make it a matter of policy to rejuvenate people in R&D by providing periodic opportunities to take on new challenges in related fields of science and technology, in project management, or in line management. They readily rotate people between undertaking R&D and managing R&D; their dual-ladder system is designed to accommodate passage from one to the other.

Motivating through Partnership

The director of strategic planning for a large, diversified company described in detail the evolving role of R&D management in the development of business and corporate strategy at her company and the hard lessons the company has learned. It is an instructive story.

Five years earlier, business managers alone developed strategy. R&D played its role by helping to implement strategy by organizing research and development to achieve the objectives set by the business managers.

A number of magnificent central research facilities served as centers of excellence in new and advanced technologies, equally as competent as the best university research centers. Their role was to stay abreast of the latest developments by doing fundamental and advanced applied research and thus to ensure that the company had the necessary capabilities to apply these developments should the company decide to use them. The central laboratories also explored a number of technological diversifications that looked promising (it was too early to include these in the strategy-development process).

Each key business that was large enough and profitable had its own R&D service center, funded by the business unit concerned. Each R&D center reported to its respective business manager. Furthermore, each of the main divisions had its own R&D facility as a service center in support of smaller businesses that could not afford to maintain their own facilities. These centers reported to their respective division managers.

All R&D used to be funded through a levy on corporate, divisional, and business-unit profits, until the company realized that many of its laboratories—not just the central ones—were engaged in work that was unrelated to the business and some even refused to respond to business-unit requests, claiming that they did not fit the laboratory's areas of interest. The company put an end to that by decreeing that the business-unit and divisional laboratories had to cover their costs by getting their internal clients to commission and pay for services rendered. It hoped in this way to ensure that, at the operating level, all R&D undertaken would be responsive to business needs and realities. The company found that implementation of the new policy contributed to discontinuing a number of far-out projects that probably would not have done much good, but it also had two negative effects.

The first, which the company vaguely expected, was that the emphasis of R&D shifted dramatically toward ensuring short-term results and away from longer-term work involving significant uncertainty. However, the company felt it could afford some movement in that direction since it still conducted some visionary R&D in its central laboratories.

What the company did not anticipate was the devastating effect the policy had on the managers and the people of R&D in the central and divisional laboratories. These laboratories lost quite a few good people from R&D to other functions within the company and to other companies; morale within R&D dropped dramatically; and the whole R&D recruiting effort was badly hurt.

One painful lesson slowly learned was that funding is a blunt instrument of policy and must be used sensitively, that it is worse than demotivating to ask R&D people to pass the beggar's bowl around. Another lesson was that it is nearly impossible to instill a sense of commercialism into R&D managers by suddenly requiring them to sell their services when they have no true sense of what their clients need or what their own services are worth or how to value them.

Having learned these lessons at substantial human and business cost, the company changed course and tackled the problem from the bottom up as well as from the top down. It required every business-unit manager to include, as a full-fledged member of the business team, a qualified representative of R&D, thus giving R&D direct access to its internal customers. It required that the same practices be instituted at the divisional level. And it made its corporate R&D director a member of the management board. The company gave the R&D representatives at each level influence over funding and a strong voice in setting targets and priorities, and it made them accountable to challenge the technological choices of the business, divisional, and corporate managers. Similarly, it made business-unit managers responsible for managing the technologies important to their businesses. All of these actions raised the profile of technology and technology management in the company to new heights.

Furthermore, the company made its project managers full partners with the R&D line managers in managing R&D projects, signaling the importance it attached to management and to the project as the primary unit of work in R&D and to management as the glue that brings people together to work toward a common objective. It then found, to its great satisfaction, that the resulting continuing dialogue at all levels between the people of R&D and the people of the business had a powerful salutary effect on motivation. The people of R&D responded positively to the trust placed in them, to their recognition as equals, and to the challenge of the new and heavy responsibility placed on their function. The company discovered a number of new truths that it was actively turning into instruments of policy:

- R&D output is enhanced by a sense of partnership with the enterprise and the combination of morale and flexibility to match skills and capabilities with needs.
- Morale in R&D is a function of doing challenging work in a rewarding environment.
- Challenging work derives from meaningful targets and rejuvenating variety.
- A rewarding environment results from the ability to influence the choice of targets, from recognition, and from trust.
- Purpose provides the opportunity for both challenging work and a rewarding environment.
- Freedom to influence purpose will be at least as motivating, if not more so, than unbridled technical freedom.

This company no longer worries about the questions concerning motivating rewards enumerated at the beginning of this chapter. The company now recognizes that the answers are not cases of either/or—rewarding individuals or teams; immediately or in the future; public recognition or money; bonuses also or standard compensation only; a share of royalties or freedom to publish; promotion or freedom of choice. The answers are some of each and some of all.

Chapter 10

The Third Generation Company

The drive for improvement never ends. The best culture, systems, and plans do not remain best for long. Economic conditions, competitors' behavior, market dynamics, technological advances, and the political environment demand changes in the most thoughtful plans.

The capacity for and openness to change are key sources of strength in corporate and business plans. And because third generation R&D management plans do not stand alone but are integral to corporate and business plans, flexibility and adaptability must also characterize the R&D component of corporate plans.

Plans must be robust enough and management insightful enough to avoid (1) needless and fruitless twists and turns in response to ill-considered threats or opportunities, (2) short-term but arresting aberrations in the environment, and (3) a predisposition toward fear when the numbers for a financial quarter don't work out as expected. Jerking R&D around in shortsighted response to short-term conditions is particularly destructive. There must be steadiness of course.

But even if adaptability can be prudent, good planning principles are stable for much longer than the plans themselves. If ensuring the conformity of all actions with environmental regulations is a corporate planning principle, the principle is unlikely to change even if business conditions or the regulations themselves change. So it is with the third generation planning principles espoused in this book: they will remain stable and constructive even as they allow change in the plans they support.

Two years have passed since Intercontinental embarked on its course toward embodying third generation R&D management.

The CEO decides that it is time to review accomplishments in the integration of R&D as a strategic force for competitive position. He wants to test the corporation's new planning philosophy, to affirm what is right, and to identify and correct what is not.

He charges his chief technology officer and a small cross-section   175 of executives from the businesses to prepare the evaluation. The "Situation Analysis," as the group calls the evaluation, runs like this:

> The situation two years earlier was characterized by a series of failures.

Communications Failures

- The absence of a common language for effective communication between businesses and R&D. That failure was the foundation of mutual misunderstanding and even distrust.

Strategic Failures

- Failure by the businesses to understand the potential strategic impact of R&D on their future competitive strength, and failure by R&D to orient its work for fullest benefit to strategic business positions.
- Although some profitable R&D results were forthcoming, they were incorporated in the business opportunistically.
- Some R&D technical successes were rejected by the businesses for lack of relevance, lowering morale in R&D and further pushing R&D to isolate itself and define its own criteria of worth.
- There was little differentiation of the types of technologies in which R&D should or should not invest.
- There was little recognition of the need for portfolio considerations; for balance in the key strategic dimensions of time, risk, uncertainty, competitive impact, inventiveness, and strategic merit; and for ensuring a full pipeline of profitable R&D results.

Operational Failures

- Project selection was driven by the resources available rather than by the merit of the individual proposals or their value in a portfolio context.
- Patchy project-management practices, occasionally excellent and sometimes haphazard.
- A pervasive uncertainty among R&D professionals about their standing in the businesses and the corporation, lack

of clarity about advancement opportunities and about the definition of personal success. This led to further retreat into the protective cocoon of the functional centers, where the R&D professionals felt understood and felt that their contributions were valued.

■ Inadequate recognition of the relationship between R&D projects that had different objectives but were supported by common technologies.

Despite those commonplace shortcomings, the business performance of the Haber Food Ingredients Division by all conventional measures was good. Growth in revenues consistently exceeded three or four times GNP. By industry standards, margins were superior. By and large, customers held high opinions of Haber's products and the division's responsiveness to their needs. The division produced much more cash than it consumed. The division's executives had reason to feel a sense of pride, and the executives of Intercontinental had reason to applaud and reward them.

But trouble was lurking behind every favorable number.

A Japanese company was threatening the profitability of vanillin, and the attack by many competitors on flavor concentrates, difficult to differentiate, continued unabated.

Because patent expiration was not far away, Haber's strong position in flavor essences was inevitably the subject of discussion in competitors' conference rooms. And the fine margins garnered by Sweetane and Enzyme Alpha, for similar reasons, would not be fine for many more years.

Always there are competitors that, lacking technological inventiveness of their own, imitate and exploit the inventiveness of the leading companies. That is a legitimate business strategy for some companies, but not for Intercontinental and for its Haber division.

Haber's chosen role was one of leadership, and Haber was primed to enjoy the fruits and endure the vicissitudes of leadership. A leadership strategy demands excellence in every function of the organization, certainly including R&D. Two years earlier, the R&D strategic component of Haber was good but not excellent. Indeed, the very success of Haber obscured the need for excellence from R&D. Perhaps Haber's success induced a certain complacency about the role of R&D. Everything looked good. Why change?

A new CEO, equipped with a sense of leadership and long-term responsibility—and a vision—forced rejection of complacency. He drove his often reluctant managers to a new level of thinking about the future. He emphasized investment in the many determinants of future prosperity not fully addressed by his predecessor. He drove the purposeful and strategic integration of R&D within those determinants.

The "Situation Analysis" concludes that there have been some significant, if still incomplete, accomplishments:

1. Introduction of a shared language through such mechanisms as joint R&D/business work groups and training programs for R&D and business managers
2. Making the technology implications of business plans and new contributions from technology to business plans more strategic through an iterative and interactive top-down/bottom-up approach
3. Characterization of all projects above a threshold of importance
4. Introduction of new R&D planning tools for R&D and the divisions:
   - Portfolio evaluation and management
   - Performance evaluation and reward systems
   - Systematic identification of shared technologies across business and division boundaries
   - Corporatewide R&D controlling and MIS systems
5. Adoption of a new philosophy:
   - A partnership approach
   - Pressure on the R&D pipeline—having more ideas than resources, always having a choice, and recognizing the value of time

From all of this, the committee compiles a summary of the results of the new planning process. In a number of areas there has been exciting progress.

- Two years brought shared understanding of certain terms, expressions, and concepts: incremental, radical, and fundamental; uncertainty and risk; risk-adjusted reward; portfolio balance; and R&D as one of the engines of future strategic condition. The role of time as a planning dimension was clarified. R&D understood better the value of the time variable in delivering results and the businesses better grasped the relationship between time to usable R&D output, the nature of the R&D task, and the R&D resources deployed for the task.

- Almost everybody is enthusiastic about the progress made toward the introduction of clear project proposals. Objectives, approaches, and required resources are now much more sharply identified, jointly by R&D project leaders, their customers in divisions, and R&D resource managers. This is even appreciated for radical and fundamental R&D, where the old beliefs that planning is impossible and will do little good are fading because of the strategic differences between incremental, radical, and fundamental R&D and the need for different approaches to manage each are now broadly understood.

- Each significant R&D project is now considered not only on its own merits but as a constituent of a strategically evaluated R&D portfolio. Portfolio characterizations and evaluations are seen both at the level of each division and for the corporation as a whole. The portfolio concept reveals strategic relationships and gaps never before recognized. Instead of the previous project-by-project approval process, the division and the corporation now apply strategic portfolio criteria to planning. They are still new and imperfectly applied, and the benefits are still not fully realized; but most people are cautiously enthusiastic about their impact on the businesses' current and future strategic condition.

- What the CEO particularly appreciates is that managers are talking much more about technology issues and that they are doing so across organizational and functional boundaries. Even business-unit directors with a relatively low affinity for technology raise the main technology challenges for their business and convincingly link them to their R&D and technology investment programs.

- Project leaders and their clients report improvements in efficiency and effectiveness:

    The share of "first-time-right" approaches has increased because of clearer targets and more joint reflection up front.

    A number of projects have been discontinued for good and well-communicated cause.

    People perceive a higher sense of urgency.

- Quality of work has taken on new meaning. The expression no longer refers only to the scientifically sound and exciting but also to timeliness and commercial value.
- Contrary to fears some expressed about stifling creativity, the R&D staff feels that planning has elevated their sense of importance and value to the company. They show a commitment to research success for the business instead of to please their R&D managers. There is less defensiveness and less tension in the R&D organization even though it is more exposed and expectations are high and clear.
- Setting up the backbone of the new planning infrastructure turned out to be rather easy from an organizational point of view.

Were these sufficient and adequate accomplishments? Of course not. The process never ends. The challenge never ceases. The accomplishments are not yet institutionalized, a part of the Intercontinental culture. They still demand reinforcement from management in the form of leadership, encouragement, pressure, and demand. The accomplishments are still reversible. In his dark moments, the CEO wonders what would happen to the new course if he were no longer around to guide it.

The analysis recognizes that the most fundamental improvements sought by Intercontinental were cultural, in the intangibles of how people think, more than in process. Process and language are vital facilitators, but the most fundamental changes have to be in the minds, spirits, and interactions of a community of people. Some people embrace change, and some are intimidated by it.

It is not surprising to the CEO's committee that some elements of success are still incompletely understood and incorporated and some are quietly opposed. The analysis summarizes those negatives:

Strategic: Strategic priority setting and resource allocation are still young, and the culture is not yet comfortable with the results of contested decisions, expressed in these terms:

To say "no" to the business clients of R&D in a division is problematic because the "higher corporate good" that gives priority to other projects has little relevance to them.
It is difficult to keep the portfolio in balance in a continuum

of change. Managers are still learning to manage with new and complex portfolio dimensions instead of individual projects.

Project management: The capabilities of project and resource managers vary considerably.

Difficulties in unlearning old habits: In several parts of the organization, the committee observes the management of R&D in several different modes—the old mode, the new mode, and the way in which the clients in the divisions would like the system to work.

The right inputs for the right decisions: Planning groups still see some decision making based on politics and resource limitations.

Flexibility: Building flexibility into plans is still incompletely expressed in excessively rigorous planning of resources and in too much detail.

Visibility traumas: Success or failure in R&D are much more visible now. The recognition of success is, of course, applauded, but an environment still needs to be created in which a well-founded decision to stop a project, if it has been competently carried out, is not considered a personal failure.

When the report is complete and all but the CTO have departed, the CEO turns to the CTO.

"Well?" he asks.

The CTO offers a summary review of the experience of the past two years.

"Given that we started to change several aspects of a complex organization simultaneously—structure, processes, support tools such as information systems, the 'mindset' of the researchers and their customers in the divisions, and, most important, culture—we are doing well. Of course, opportunities exist to do even better.

"The most important outcome of the last two years has been a change in the way our managers think. It is not the planning principles or concepts that have been important. They are merely tools. I hope you noticed that people now express themselves instinctively in terms of R&D strategy, the R&D portfolio, and the strategic impact of the R&D portfolio of their businesses.

"But we need to propel this way of thinking to a new level of steadiness, to institutionalize it. Today it is still fragile and tentative.

"To make the R&D management process more practicable and acceptable we have to recognize that generating the information we need to assess projects and project ideas takes time and requires the extensive involvement of functional managers in the businesses and in R&D. Several of them have approached me to say that their time is not well spent because we are asking for too much, and too early in the project's life cycle. Given that a growing number of their colleagues feel we are doing things at the right level of detail, and that linking R&D projects to a business perspective needs to be done as early as possible, I still bet that the continued learning process will win most managers over.

"We can and should be more selective, however, by focusing the portfolio treatment more on the projects that are more important for Intercontinental. Important does not only refer to the projects' size. What matters particularly is the strategic importance of projects in terms of the business consequences of success or failure, the scarcity of the R&D resources we have to use on the projects, and the need to focus more on marginal projects that merit special management attention.

"For example, the large Enzyme Beta project clearly should continue to receive portfolio attention because of its size and its strategic potential. But we must keep an eye on the still-small radical projects because, if successful, they will require resource commitments of many millions of dollars. Also, the vanillin cost-reduction project should be continually reexamined in the portfolio context because we are facing major market and competitive uncertainties that could kill it.

"Another area that requires simplification is reporting. Since all R&D produces is knowledge, the reporting of that knowledge is important. However, it should not be necessary to report the same thing two or three times. Some R&D managers now report at project milestones, for the quarterly department reports, and for the quarterly R&D reports to the divisions. By reporting both in the old mode of quarterly reports and in the new mode of milestones, and by too much willingness to lean over backward and provide the divisions with all the information they want, R&D wastes a lot of effort. Let's streamline and focus on milestone reports.

"The next area we have to give more attention to is quality in all areas involving projects—project proposals, project-team composition, execution, and reporting. When we put the spotlight on the project managers two years ago, we did not do enough to mobilize the talent of the line managers in support of the projects. As a consequence, we see that in several R&D departments the content, progress, and challenge of projects are inadequately discussed. As a consequence we sometimes do not get the most appropriate people to work on a project, and we see great differences in the quality of project proposals and execution.

"I propose that we dedicate more time in our R&D management group meetings to frank discussions about projects, particularly the ones that require the involvement of people from different departments. This will help the managers to learn from each other and to calibrate the deployment of the technology management support tools. We are not trying to allocate blame for suboptimal performance. We want to learn from each other by continuing to encourage openness and trust."

"What you have suggested sounds like common sense," the CEO says. "What keeps surprising me, though, is the effort and time it takes to introduce these kinds of things at Intercontinental. What else is on your action list?"

"An important area that we have to give more consideration to is the portfolio-balancing process, as opposed to the quality of the individual projects and project ideas that make up the portfolio. I believe that fine-tuning is needed in several components: the involvement of the right people, the rating of projects at the division and corporate levels, the control and discipline we apply to the review and restructuring of the project portfolio, and communicating to all the rationale for our decisions."

"I like that," the CEO responds. "You see, I am still not satisfied with the polite, political decision making that seems to be taking place when we review the portfolios for the whole of Intercontinental. Sometimes, it seems to me that the power of the participants better explains the acceptance and priority of a project than its merit. We also seem to treat budgeted projects as sacrosanct, and we still do not feel comfortable with multiyear commitments. On the other hand, I agree that we have come a long way in two years. Projects are much clearer and more accessible for senior managers, and much more attention is paid to business and corporate strategy in making the trade-offs. Do we need any more changes?"

"When we look at the portfolio-balancing process, we see two weak links," the CTO says.

"First, programs aimed at diversification or fundamental discovery do not get a fair chance because they normally do not have a champion of equal strength compared to the champions within the existing businesses.

"Second, regarding the discipline we apply to the review and the restructuring of the portfolio, we have to keep hammering on a few important rules:

- Portfolio choices are governed by business and corporate strategy.
- Budgeted work is not sacrosanct; it can be suspended or terminated when business conditions change or when better project proposals come up.
- Project ideas should get attention at any time, not just at budget time.
- There should always be an 'overbook,' a backlog of projects and ideas.
- Licensing and purchasing technology must constantly be considered as an alternative, not as a last resort.

"The most important lesson is that effective R&D planning is doable, profitable, and ongoing. True, it demands leadership, insight, and effort; it needs a lot of time from you and your managers, as well as from those they manage. The lesson is that there is no simple formula for success, but there are guiding principles whose application, though demanding, is rewarding beyond the hopes of the planners."

"Not bad," the CEO smiles. "Not bad at all. But the long-distance runner has only completed his first lap."

"True, but he is in the lead, and he is showing signs of endurance," the CTO replies.

"We will endure, because it is exciting to be leaders," the CEO says.

"And that is what we get paid for," the CTO concludes.

AFTERWORD

Intercontinental is a composite company. The conversations that develop the themes of this book are constructs to facilitate communication of those themes and recognition of the human dimensions that are the source of constructive change and of resistance to it. Nevertheless, the Intercontinental case presents real problems faced by real companies in many industries, and the need for the purposeful and strategic management of R&D—that is, for third generation R&D management—in most of these companies is painfully evident.

Only with the leadership and energy of the most senior management of a company can third generation R&D management be established. For companies whose success relies in significant measure on R&D, the effectiveness of the most senior executives in R&D management—their success at securing the cooperation and support of their people—is a key determinant of whether the company will prosper. We know that the principles, tools, and practices of third generation R&D management, creatively applied by determined executive leaders in partnership across the company, greatly enhance the likelihood of continued corporate success.

The test of the value of this book is whether readers not only understand its messages but feel equipped to act on them "on Monday morning," as it were. We hope a course of action is now clear to each reader, but a recapitulation may be useful. Senior executives might start by asking themselves these questions:

- How important is R&D to my company's various businesses?
- How effective is our integration of R&D, business, and corporate strategy?
- What is the quality of our plans' balance in time, risk, reward, competitive impact, and the many other dimensions of strategic merit?
- How good is the spirit of partnership between R&D and the company's other functional communities?

The answers to those questions will define the next actions to take.
   Less senior managers in all functions across the company should
ask the same questions and add to the list one more:

- How can I get my boss to read this book, grasp these ideas,
  and make third generation R&D management happen in this
  company?

INDEX

Academic research, 24, 25, 126f
Accountability, 28, 120–121
AIRBUS consortium, 129
Akzo (company), 133f
Allen, T. J., 158
Antitrust laws, 129
Apple Computer, 14–15, 56
Aspartame, 29
AT&T, 56, 126f
Automated teller machine (ATM) industry, 13–14

Back burner projects, 145
Backlog of ideas, 152f, 155–156, *184*
Base technology, 64f, 127
Bayer (Germany), 56
Becton Dickinson, 135
Biotechnology, 59–61
Boehringer Ingelheim, 125–126, 131, 133, 134–135
Bootleg research, 145–146, 149–150
Bristol-Myers Squibb, 128
Business-business collaboration, 129–130
Business portfolio, 93

Capital investment, 95f, 97f
Career development, 166–167
Centralization/decentralization issue, 130–135
  and company size, 132f
CEO. *See also* Senior management
  early role in R&D projects and, *84, 85f, 85–86*
  implementation issues and, 123
  tyranny of the calendar and, 79
  utility of planning principles and, 67–79
  views of R&D, 41–43
Chemical industry, 133f
Chief technology officer (CTO), 42, 167
Churchill, Winston, 118–119
Ciba-Geigy, 133f
Client relationship, 159–160, *179–180. See also* Customer service; Supplier/customer relationship
Commodity products, 48, *68f*

Communication
  common vocabulary and, 77, 79, 94, 151, 152f, 153, 165, *178*
  decentralization and, 130–131
  failures of, 176
  in first generation R&D management, 26
  at Intercontinental, *43–45, 77, 79, 178, 183*
  among operating functions, 6, 10, 148
  in second generation R&D management, 30, 35
  in third generation R&D management, 37, 147–148, *183*
Competitive advantage, durability of, 95f, 96, 97f
Competitive characteristics, 47–53
Competitive impact, 64f, 64–65, 65f, 87
  R&D portfolio and, 94, 95f, *106, 108f*
Competitive threat, 69–70
Consolidation, 119–120
Continuity, 28, 32, 175
Corporate culture, 164–165, *180*
Cost. *See* Capital investment; Risk/reward relationship
Cost/benefit assessment, 27, 32, 38
Cost centers, 26, 27
Costs vs. risks, 75
Cost-to-completion, 95f, 96, 97f
Creativity, 29, 90–91, 96, 150, 180
  as trait, 169, 170
Customer service, 46–47, 53. *See also* Client relationship

DARPA. *See* Defense Advanced Research Projects Administration
DCF. *See* Discounted-cash-flow (DCF) calculations
Decentralization
  pressures for, 133–135
  strengths and weaknesses of, 130–131, 131f
Defense Advanced Research Projects Administration (DARPA), 129
Development, 14, 148
Discounted-cash-flow (DCF) calculations, 97

Page references followed by a lower case "f" refer to figures; those in italic refer to the fictional "Intercontinental Company, Inc."

187

Dithering, 144
Drucker, Peter, 3, 153
DSM (Holland), 56, 126f, 128, 133f
Du Pont, 56, 89, 133f

EC. *See* European Commission
Edison, Thomas, 150
Edsel projects, 145
Electronic watch, 63
European Commission (EC), 126f, 128–129
Evaluation. *See* Cost/benefit assessment;
    Progress evaluation; Results, measure-
    ment of
Existing business, 17, *184*
Exposure, 95f
External R&D linkages, 126–130, 166–167,
    184

Failure
    fear of, 150
    uncertainty and, 167
Familiarity index. *See* Marketing
Feasibility study, *82–84*, 91
First generation R&D management, 6–7
    characteristics of, 25–30, 31f
    at Intercontinental, *44*
    operating principles, 28–30
    organization in, 27–28, 31f, 138
Flexibility, 40, *181*
Formulation technology, *49–50*
Foster, Richard, 64
Fuji, 89
Fundamental R&D, 16–17
    centralization and, 132
    characteristics of, 54f, *57f*
    in first generation R&D management, 29
    project uncertainty and, *81–82*
    risk and, *73–75*
    in second generation R&D management,
        32, 33
    strategic factors in investment in, *55–56,*
        86
    in third generation R&D management, 38
Funding
    of academic research, 24, 25
    in first generation R&D management, 26,
        27, 28, 31f, 111
    historical changes in, 24–25
    at Intercontinental, *43*, *44*
    as policy instrument, 171–172
    in second generation R&D management,
        33, 36f
    in third generation R&D management, 38,
        39f, 111

GE, 89
General management. *See also* CEO; Senior
    management
    in first generation R&D management, 26
    R&D wants vs. resource constraints and,
        23, 24f
    in second generation R&D management,
        30
    in third generation R&D management, 35
    views of R&D, 41–42, *181*
Globalization, 131
Government-business collaboration,
    128–129

Haber Food Ingredients Division, *45–47*
    business strategies by product cluster, *68f,*
        70f, 71f, 74f
    common vocabulary issue at, *153*
    portfolio decisions at, *112–121*
    portfolio planning process at, *98–112*
    R&D portfolio dimensions at, *100f*
    sales, margins, and profits by product, *47f*
    situation analysis at, *175–184*
Hamel, Gary, 6–7
Harvard University, 128
HDTV (High-definition television), 129
Hoechst, 56, 128

IBM, 14, 35, 56, 126f, 129
ICI, 56, 128
Incremental R&D, 15
    centralization and, 132
    characteristics of, 54f, *57f*
    in first generation R&D management, 27,
        29
    at Haber, *54–55, 57f, 68–69, 80–81*
    planning and, *68–69*
    project uncertainty and, *80–81*
    in second generation R&D management,
        32, 33
    in third generation R&D management, 38
Industry cycle, mission of R&D and, 18–21,
    19f
Information system, 157, *178*
Information technology, 131
Ingersoll-Rand, 10
Input/output orientation, 135–139
Integration
    corporate R&D issues and, *119–120*
    interfacial linkages and, 148
    at project level, 10, 30, 32
Intercontinental Company, Inc. *See also* Ha-
    ber Food Ingredients Division; Medelec-
    tronics Division

organization of, *42f, 43*
strategic discussion at, *45–57*
Interdisciplinary teams, 160
Intuitive mode. *See* First generation R&D
    management
Inventive merit, 95f, 96, 97f
Investment portfolio, 93–94

Japan, 3, 5, 128
Joint objectives, development of, 153–155

Katz, R., 158
Key technology, 64f, 127
Knowledge
    implementation of, 67
    state-of-the-art, 79–82

Leadership, *119,* 147–148
    radical R&D and, *71–72, 78*
Leadership position, corporate, 90, *177*
Lead-time reduction, 2, 148–149. *See also*
    Time-to-completion
Line organization, 139, 141f, 159, 173
Lost projects, 145

Make-or-buy decision, 127, 130
Management. *See* CEO; General manage-
    ment; Project management; R&D man-
    agers; Senior management
Management context
    dispersed R&D and, 134–135
    in first generation R&D management,
        26–28, 31f
    in second generation R&D management,
        32–33, 36f
    in third generation R&D management,
        35–38, 39f
Management philosophy
    in first generation R&D management,
        26–27, 31f
    in second generation R&D management,
        32, 32–33, 36f
    in third generation R&D management, 35,
        37, 39f, *178*
Manufacturing cost reduction, 15, *48,*
    54–55, 68–69. See also Incremental
    R&D
Marketing, 95f, 97f, *106, 109f, 115, 118f,*
    156–157
Market intelligence gap, 34
Massachusetts General Hospital, 128
Massachusetts Institute of Technology
    (MIT), 126f, 128

Matrix management, 32, 139–140, 140f,
    141f, 159–161
Medelectronics Division, R&D needs of, *73,*
    86
Merck, 35
Milestone reporting, *182*
Military-industrial R&D, 24
Misfits, 143–144
Mishaps, 143, 144
MIT. *See* Massachusetts Institute of Tech-
    nology
Mobility of staff, 166, 167–168
Monsanto, 56
Montedison-Himont, 56
Morale, 172, 173
Morita, Akio, 3, 5
Motivation, 163–173, *178*
    human traits of R&D people and,
        168–171
    matching resources with needs and,
        165–168
    through partnership, 171–173
Motorola, 129–130

NEC, 56, 89
Net-present-value (NPV) calculations, 96–97
New business, 18
Nothing-better-to-do projects, 146
NPV. *See* Net-present-value (NPV) calcula-
    tions

Obstacles, 9–11
Old, Bruce, 1
Operating principles. *See also* Strategic plan-
    ning principles
    in first generation R&D management,
        28–30, 31f
    in second generation R&D management,
        33–35, 36f
    in third generation R&D management, 39f
Organization
    centralization vs. decentralization and,
        130–135
    in first generation R&D management,
        27–28, 31f
    input- vs. output-orientation and,
        135–139, 137f
    internal vs. external resources and,
        126–130
    issues of, 124f
    project-team structure and, 152f, 158–161
    responsiveness to change and, 125–126

Organization (*continued*)
  in second generation R&D management, 32–33, 36f
  structural elements of, 126
  suboptimal, 123–124
  in third generation R&D management, 37, 39f, 123–142

Pacing technology, 64f
Partnership approach, 35–37, 171–173, *178*
Pasteurization, 60–61
Patent security, *71, 177*
Performance evaluation, 167, *178*
Personality traits of managers and R&D people, 168–171
Personnel. *See* Motivation
Pert and Gantt charts, 157
Pharmaceutical industry, 125–126, 128
Philips (company), 126f, 129
Prahalad, C. K., 6–7
Priority setting
  in first generation R&D management, 29, 31f
  problems with, *180–181*
  process for, 152f, 153–155
  in second generation R&D management, 33–34, 36f
  in third generation R&D management, 38, 39f
Probability of success, 95f, 97f, *104f*
Product clusters
  business strategies by, *68f, 70f, 71f, 74f*
  R&D needs and, 47–53
Progress evaluation, 157
  in first generation R&D management, 29–30, 31f
  in second generation R&D management, 34, 36f
  in third generation R&D management, 39f, 40, 143
Project attractiveness
  elements of, *94, 95f*
  ranking of elements in, 96, 97f, 97–98
  R&D portfolio and, 94–96
Project-by-project management, 7–8, 30, 33, 113, 130. *See also* Second generation R&D management
Project level integration, 10, 30, 32
Project management
  in first generation R&D management, 27–28
  input- vs. output-orientation of structure and, 136, 138

key practices for, 151–161
objectives of senior management in, 146–151, 152f
organization structure and, 139, 141f, 158–161
problems with, *181*
project budget and, 160
in second generation R&D management, 32–33
Project plan, 157
Project-team structure, 152f, 158–161
Project termination, 150–151, 155–156, *179, 181, 184*
Purposeful mode. *See* Third generation R&D management

Quality, *180, 182–183*

Radical R&D, 15–16, *55*
  centralization and, 132
  characteristics of, 54f, 57f
  in first generation R&D management, 27, 29
  project uncertainty and, *80, 81*
  risk and, *70–73*
  in second generation R&D management, 32, 33
  in third generation R&D management, 38
RCA, 126f, 129
R&D
  basic types of, 15–17, *53–54, 54f, 57f. See also* Fundamental R&D; Incremental R&D; Radical R&D
  historical changes in environment for, 24–25
  joint, 126f, 126–130
  problems with visibility of, *181*
  strategic mission of, *65*
  strategic purposes of, 17–21
  symptoms of problems in, 144–146
R&D accountability, 120–121
R&D budget, *43, 44*
  familiarity of technologies and markets analysis, *109f*
  portfolio balance and, *100, 101f*
  project by competitive impact analysis, *108f*
  project by time-to-completion analysis, *107f*
  reward by probability of success analysis, *104f*
  technological maturity by competitive strength analysis, *102f*

R&D managers
  evaluation of project attractiveness and,
    109–111
  in first generation R&D management,
    26–27
  strategic business concerns and, 10, 78–79
  in third generation R&D management, 37
R&D portfolio, 93–121, 179
  decision process for, 112–119
  project attractiveness and, 94–98
  review process and, 99–112, 154, 178, 184
  strategic balance in, 54, 86, 99–112, 182,
    183–184
  strategic matrices, 102f, 104f, 107f, 108f,
    109f
  strategic relevance of, 95f, 96
  technological maturity and, 94, 102f, 103
R&D strategy cycle, 20f
Recruiting, 165–167
Reengineering, 145
Reporting by milestones, 182
Reporting relationships, 159
Reprioritization, 144
Research, defined, 14
Resource allocation
  crisis mode of, 144
  in first generation R&D management, 26,
    27, 28–29, 31f
  process for, 152f, 153–155, 155f
  in second generation R&D management,
    33–34, 36f
  technological competitive strength and,
    90–91
  in third generation R&D management, 38,
    39f, 40, 151
Resource availability, 37
Resource constraints, vs. management wants,
    23, 24f
Results
  management for, 146–161
  measurement of, 5–6, 26, 31f, 34, 36f, 37,
    39f, 40
  organization for, 123–142
  short- vs. long-term, 75
  of strategic planning process, 178–180
Reward system. See Motivation
Rhône-Poulenc, 56
Risk
  commercial, 72–73
  definition of, 76–77
  factors in, 50–52
  failures of omission and, 74
  fundamental R&D and, 73–75

incremental R&D and, 69–70
  radical R&D and, 16, 70–73
  reconceptualization of uncertainty as, 77,
    79, 82–86
  technological, 72, 80
  vs. uncertainty, 75–77
Risk/reward relationship
  exploratory phase and, 82
  R&D investments and, 77–78, 78f
  R&D portfolio and, 93, 95f, 97f, 98,
    103–105, 104f, 113, 116f
  responsibility for decisions on, 75
Roberts, Edward, 84
Rotation
  into R&D, 166, 167–168
  within R&D, 171

Schlatter, James, 29
Schon, Donald A., 76
Second generation R&D management, 7–8
  characteristics of, 30–35, 36f
  organization in, 32–33, 36f, 138
Senior management. See also CEO; General
    management; R&D managers
  course of action for, 185–186
  familiarity with technology, 9–10, 164
  key practices for, 151–161
  role of, 3, 5, 9, 143, 146–151
Sensory resource, 49
Shapiro, Irving, 44
Siemens, 56, 126f, 129, 134
Situation analysis, 175–184
Sony, 14, 56
State-of-the-art knowledge, 79–82, 135–136
Steele, Lowell, 3, 8, 9
Strategic context
  in first generation R&D management, 28,
    31f
  in second generation R&D management,
    32–33, 36f
  in third generation R&D management,
    35–38, 39f
Strategic planning
  accomplishments of, 175–180
  implementation process and, 153–155, 154f
  negative experiences from, 180–181
  relevant questions in, 56, 106
  survival of enterprise and, 78
Strategic planning principles, 53–57, 59–65,
    175. See also Competitive impact; Proj-
    ect attractiveness; Technological com-
    petitive strength; Technological maturity
Strategic relevance, 95f, 96

Strategy of hope, 6–7. *See also* First generation R&D management
Structural interfaces, linking of, 148
Supplier/customer relationship, 30, 32

Tagamet (antiulcer drug), 63
Targeting
in first generation R&D management, 29, 31f
in second generation R&D management, 36f
in third generation R&D management, 37–38, 39f
Teams
interdisciplinary, 160
project-team structure, 152f, 158–161
Technical talent, 1–2, 134
Technological competitive impact. *See* Competitive impact
Technological competitive strength, 87–91
external R&D resources and, 127
R&D portfolio and, 94, 102f, 103, 113, 114f
resource allocation and, 90–91
technological maturity and, 88–89, 102f
template for determination of, 88f
Technological maturity, 49–50, 59–64, 87
characteristics of R&D as function of, 63f
concept of, 59–62
curve of, 61f, 62f
generalized characteristics of, 63f
organization structure and, 141f
R&D portfolio and, 94, 102f, 103
strategic planning and, 62–64
technological competitive strength and, 88–89, 102f
Technological uncertainty
aggressive "shoot" approach to, 152f, 156–157
R&D portfolio and, 106, 109f
reduction of, 84
technological maturity and, 60
Technology
aging of, and new technologies, 63–64
communication of importance of, 167, 179
competitive impact of, 64f, 64–65
defined, 13
in first generation R&D management, 28, 29, 31f
rate of change in, 138–139
role of R&D in deepening of capabilities in, 18

in second generation R&D management, 33, 34, 36f
in third generation R&D management, 37, 38, 39f
"Technology manager," 130. *See also* Chief technology officer
Third generation R&D management
characteristics of, 35–40, 39f
characterization of, 3, 4f
concept of, 8–9
key practices of, 151–161
objectives of, 146–151, 152f
organization in, 37, 39f, 138–139
roots of, 5–9
Thomson (company), 126f, 129
3M company, 29
Time
as planning dimension, 178–179
progression of competitive impact over, 64, 65f
Time-to-completion, 95f, 96, 97f, 105–106, 107f, 113, 115, 117f. *See also* Lead-time reduction
Toshiba, 129–130
Toyobo, 126f
Toyota, 89
Training programs, 178
Transparency, 149–150

Uncertainty. *See also* Technological uncertainty
CEO and, 41–42
R&D portfolio and, 95f, 105
reconceptualized as risk, 77, 79, 82–86
vs. risk, 75–77
sharing of, 149–150
U.S. Memories, Inc., 129
University-industry cooperation, 127–128
Urgency, sense of, 148–149, 179

Vagelos, Roy, 35
Vocabulary commonality, importance of, 77, 79, 94, 151, 152f, 153, 165, 178
Von Clausewitz, Claude, 41, 57

Waste, 124
Webb, James, 44
Weisner, Jerome, 11

Yale University, 128